Confessions of a Lapsed Liberal

I've Seen the Light

NICHOLAS J. NIGRO

CRYPTIC PRESS   BRONX, N.Y.

Published by Cryptic Press Inc.
314 West 231st Street, Suite 452
Bronx, New York 10463

©1997 by Nicholas J. Nigro

All rights reserved. No part of this book may be reproduced in any form without written permission from the publisher, except where permitted by law. For more information, contact Cryptic Press Inc.

Publisher's Cataloging in Publication
(Prepared by Quality Books Inc.)

Nigro, Nicholas J.
   Confessions of a lapsed liberal: I've seen the light / Nicholas J. Nigro

   p. cm.
   Preassigned LCCN: 96-86184
   ISBN: 1-887775-41-2

   1. Liberalism. 2. United States--Social conditions. 3. United States--Politics and government. 4. Right and left (Political science) I. Title II. Title: I've seen the light

JC574.N54 1997   320.5'1
                        QBI96-40808

*In Memoriam
Six Stars Diner
They tried to survive.
Let's put it that way.*

<u>Like It Is</u>

Last year, I was laid off from a job, and filed a claim for unemployment insurance. While filling out the paperwork in my local Department of Labor office, I truthfully answered that I was an officer in a corporation licensed to do business in New York State. I was, and am, president of a small company. At that time, the company was brand-new, in the red, and paid me no salary. I still relied on a "real" job to pay my bills.

I was denied unemployment benefits because I was told I *technically* had a job. My former employer was not disputing my claim; this was a determination of *The State*. I appealed the decision, had a hearing, and their decision was upheld. The bland bureaucrat with the Caribbean lilt pronounced that "Mr. Mannion stands to gain."

Stands to gain....

In the future--*hopefully*, but for a fellow living one day at a time, I found myself with zero income and no health insurance. A Dickensian waif cast out into the cold, cruel world. This while immigrants, both legal and illegal, literally step off the boat and into welfare offices to receive free money that I, as a taxpayer, help subsidize.

I wasn't asking for a handout, just the unemployment insurance I had paid into. I left the experience having far less sympathy for those with their hands out, especially those who consider it their birthright.

It's enough to turn a fellow into a Republican....

I was penalized for trying to fulfill the *American Dream.* So much for encouraging the entrepreneurial spirit--a frequent boast of the Clinton administration. Yet when I ride the NYC subway system, I see posters encouraging businesses run by *women and minorities* to contract with NYC. And more and more ads in the classified section of *The New York Times* end with the phrase, *"Women and minorities are encouraged to respond to this ad."*

Yes, I **AM** a white male. An embattled white male trying not to become embittered.

It's not easy.

For the record, I consider myself a liberal. My definition of a liberal is someone who listens to all points of view and then makes up his mind. Someone who tries to practice a "live and let live" philosophy. Someone who tries to find what Quakers call "peace at the center."

I have known the author of *Confessions* since we met in St. John's schoolyard in 1971. I believe the above description applies to him, though today he eschews the **"L"** word with the same *passionate intensity* that he gushed over Mario Cuomo's 1984 keynote address to the Democratic National Convention.

I agree with *most* of what is written in *Confessions*. And it is written with humor, self-deprecating candor, and *malice toward some*, but certainly not *all*. It is one man's coming-of-age, coming-to-one's-senses political memoir, though in its highly personal nature, it speaks to the vast *Silent Majority*. After multitudinous metamorphoses and many flights of fancy, Nick has finally *seen the light.*

Take it fom this *liberal* — he is telling it **like it is.**

James Mannion
Bronx, New York
January 1997

In The Beginning

Time is a great teacher, but unfortunately it kills all its pupils.

--Hector Berlioz

The Rest of the Story

For those of you who have read *America Off-Line: Reagan to O.J.*, you'll probably find occasional repetition in this cathartic tome of mine. Please forgive these transgressions.

To tell the complete story of my metamorphosis from knee-jerk liberal to quasi-libertarian-conservative, I could not avoid retelling my Mario Cuomo infatuation story and a few other pertinent anecdotes.

Confessions of a Lapsed Liberal: I've Seen the Light is not the work of a biased think-tank, or a paid-in-full product of the *National Endowment for the Arts*. Rather, it's a product of a humble Bronx Kid's heart--an anecdotal journey through the *Twilight Zone* of a changing America.

Submitted then for your approval....

Who Am I, Why Am I Here?

I was born in the South Bronx when JFK was President and grew up due north in a neighborhood called Kingsbridge. It was a great place to live in the 60s and 70s, mixing a touch of suburbia with the conveniences of the city. The nearby Number One subway line was our token anywhere from the bustle of Manhattan to the shores of the Atlantic Ocean in Queens or Brooklyn.

I grew up in a two-family home, purchased by my Italian-immigrant grandparents in 1946, on a quiet block. Through 1971, across the street from the house, stood one of the last remaining Victory Gardens in the Bronx. It was a remarkable place, with a man-made well that tapped into the long-covered waters of Tibbetts Brook, still flowing beneath the earth. My grandfather, father, and various locals, planted tomatoes, peppers, eggplants, strawberries, figs, rhubarb, peaches, corn, and more. It was a veritable farm born on an empty lot. Barbecues were held there on the big holidays: Memorial Day, the Fourth of July, and Labor Day. Flags flew. Not in your face, but part of the sense of community that existed in those days. When *the Garden* was bulldozed in the name of progress, it ended, for me, one of the last vestiges of a simpler, better epoch in a changing borough, city, and country.

5 April 1995

No, I'm not dyslexic--I'm just paying homage to *ABC News*, its pompous and plasticized anchor, Peter Jennings, and his droning blowhard colleague on *Nightline*, Ted Koppel.

On this date, I went to a Barnes & Noble superstore on 21st Street in Manhattan to see the renowned writer Pete Hamill, who was touting his recently-released memoir, *A Drinking Life*. Accompanying me on this night on the town were two friends, one of whom was a debonair, pepper-haired senior citizen with a bum knee.

We thought we'd arrived early enough, but were surprised to see all the seats taken. My sixty-something buddy was forced to stand. None of the twenty or thirty-something Yuppies offered him a chair.

When Hamill finally showed, the place was teeming. He read excerpts from his book and entertained questions from the swooning throng.

"Are you still a liberal?" a woman called out.

Hamill, it should be noted, has built his

reputation primarily as a journalist and passionate defender of liberal causes. Apparently, Hamill, circa 1995, had frightened some of his fans with recent columns which indicated, perhaps, a shift in his political sentiments.

"Yes, I still am," he responded.

With that, a palpable sense of relief swept over the Manhattan crowd as they applauded. The audience wore their liberalism like a badge of honor.

When the show ended, the reassured assemblage ventured out into the *city that never sleeps*, with autographed books in hand. Many headed home to their doormanned high-rises.

My two compatriots and I returned to the Bronx.

"Are you still a liberal?" Hamill says, "Yes!"

I say, "No!"

And this is my confession. I was a liberal for some time. I voted for Mondale, Dukakis, Cuomo, and Clinton in 1992. (Clinton was the last straw--more on that later.)

How and why did this transformation occur? And where do lapsed liberals go? Read on: Find out why this formerly-enthusiastic liberal is no more.

<u>Birth of a Liberal</u>

The scuttlebutt is that colleges and universities are hotbeds of liberalism and socialism. This may be the case.

I entered Manhattan College and promptly registered a Republican when I turned eighteen. Four years later, upon graduation, I was swooning over Mario Cuomo's keynote address to the 1984 Democratic National Convention and was enthusiastic, believe it or not, about Walter Mondale's presidential candidacy.

Who did this to me? Idealistic youth and liberalism are a good fit. Adult realities and liberalism fit like Pee Wee Herman in a John Wayne movie. There is nothing compassionate about a ballooning welfare state, and government program after government program designed to break the back of poverty, and doing nothing of the kind. In fact, poverty is the only inheritance that the government lets you pass onto your heirs.

Stay tuned.

Who's The Lunkhead?

A final word on Pete Hamill. He once wrote a column condemning the people of the state of New Hampshire for participating in the American political process. Caught up in the maelstrom of political correctness, Hamill rued the fact that a predominantly white state *(God forbid!)* played a prominent role in picking our president. He referred to the *Granite State* as a place full of "fat, balding white guys wedged into diner booths." Hamill obviously has a problem with people who work for a living, pay taxes, don't commit crimes, and vote (not to mention fat, balding white men).

A Miracle Called Friendship

Nobody leaves my presence without being properly indoctrinated.
- Zeke

I've got a friend who has granted me full permission to elaborate on his unapologetic leftist political philosophy. I'll be referring to him, and quoting him throughout this book. His name is Ezekiel (his friends call him "Zeke") and he is a hard core, fortyish left-winger who, more than any other human being, has helped me escape the intellectual swamp of slavish devotion to government programs and social-engineering policies. Zeke has accomplished this by exposing the flagrant hypocrisy of modern liberalism.

Zeke was born in the small town of Voluntown, Connecticut. His father moved to Manhattan when he was a boy of twelve to become a doorman. Zeke's dad, feeling ill-used by his employer, became a socialist, voting for Henry Wallace in 1948.

Zeke is his father's son.

This past year, Zeke opted to leave his neighborhood of fifteen years because a new "element" was closing in around him. During his search for a new place to live, he considered moving into a cozy building complex in an established middle-income neighborhood. But he decided against it, when he heard that the city might be *taking over* one of the buildings. And everyone knows what that means....

What does Zeke say about all of this? He says he supports the policy of plopping *Section Eight* welfare families into middle-income buildings (with tenant populations of working people). He says he understands why it's done. He, of course, would never live there and *probably* wouldn't be for the policy if he did.

Coach

I.F. Stone...unbelievable man...
amazing human being.
- Zeke, on I.F. Stone, Josef Stalin booster

In the early 1980s Zeke coached in a junior baseball league for pubescent boys. During this coaching tenure, he labored valiantly to impart values to the youngsters on his team. Foremost, the game was a game and was to be played for fun...and Ronald Reagan was an ogre and racist, and the Soviet Union, with its universal health care, was a better place to live than these United States.

In a position of authority, Zeke set out to put his *imprimatur* on the league. Initially, his peers assumed he was just another sports-minded galoot. They were in for a rude awakening.

Zeke, you see, was firmly rooted in the compassionate liberal mind-set of the 1960s. He was, foremost, concerned only about the "feelings" of the kids.

So he tried to convince his star players to forgo participating in an annual all-star game, which pitted his league against another. Zeke told them that such a game was "exclusive," and many of their teammates would feel the pain of rejection when not chosen to participate. Good-intentions notwithstanding, Zeke was ousted faster than you can say "Peter, Paul, and Mary."

True Confessions

It is not the criminal things which are the hardest to confess, but the ridiculous....

--Rousseau, *Confessions*

The Windbag Beneath My Wings

Compassion...good word...compassion.
- Zeke

In June of 1977, Mario Cuomo was whisked into my Bronx neighborhood atop his *Cuo-Mobile*. He was in the midst of a heated battle for the New York City Democratic mayoral nomination. The diminutive Abe Beame was the unpopular incumbent.

The other serious candidates in the race were the rapidly falling star, Bella Abzug, and the *holier-than-thou* Ed Koch.

Cuomo was serving as New York Secretary of State in Governor Hugh Carey's administration. (What a *state* Secretary of State does is anybody's guess.) Koch mocked Cuomo's lack of qualifications for the mayor's job.

Standing on the Cuo-Mobile platform, Cuomo gave a little speech in front of Shelvyn's Bakery on W. 231st Street, the hub of the neighborhood. In the small crowd gathered to hear him, an oldster took exception to the candidate's position on the death penalty. Cuomo was against it.

Mario invited his detractor onto the platform to debate the issue further. He was a bully even then. Predictably, the shaken geezer declined the *opportunity.*

Still, Cuomo was impressive that day. He was more Citizen Cuomo in the 1970s. Not yet a compromised liberal politician, spewing empty rhetoric and kowtowing at the altar of political correctness.

I would have voted for Mario that year, but I was only fifteen. Without my vote, he lost to Ed Koch. (He did exact a measure of revenge in 1982, when he trounced the incumbent mayor in the Democratic primary for the state's gubernatorial nomination. And yes, I got to vote for my political hero at last.)

Governor Cuomo, as mankind knows, became an overnight sensation, peaking in popularity after his stirring keynote speech to the Democratic National Convention in 1984. Oh, if only he was the presidential nominee, us liberals swooned.

Better than anyone else in America, he defined liberalism in its most idealistic state. Regrettably, like most left-wingers, Mario's words were just that--*words!* (Ironically he has compiled his speeches in a book titled, *More Than Words.*)

As governor, he was lame. His biggest claim to fame is his having built more jails than any of his predecessors. An unusual accomplishment for the *King of Liberalism* to tout.

Admittedly, it took me a while to appreciate Cuomo's vacuousness and to recognize that he was largely hot air. He gave a great speech, brow-beat detractors with rhetorical aplomb, and often made those who disagreed with him seem asinine. Cuomo was the consummate showman--always good theater. But over time his act became tedious, especially when the reality of his listless leadership became apparent.

In 1988, Cuomo was looming large over the announced Democratic aspirants for president (called *the Seven Dwarfs*). It was Mario's year, no doubt about it. The Reagan Era was ending, and it appeared that Americans were open to electing a Democrat. Vice President Bush was the favorite on the Republican side. *Bush-Cuomo.* For us Democrats it was a dream match-up. The *fussy patrician* versus the *golden-tongued ethnic.*

True-to-form, New York's *Hamlet-on-the-Hudson* couldn't make up his mind in 88 and we got Mike Dukakis, the flip side of Cuomo. Where Cuomo was electricity, Dukakis was steam.

His indecision in 1988 marked the end-of-the-line for him as the heavy-weight champion of the national Democratic party.

He returned once more with his *Hamlet Act* in 1992, but by then Mario was *old hat*, unpopular even in New York. He lost his bid for a fourth term as governor two years later.

Where did Cuomo go wrong? What happened to that politician that impressed me so much as a teenager?

This happened: When addressing a black audience, Cuomo told them that the *only* reason Jesse Jackson wasn't the President of the United States was because of his skin color. *Reality check, Mario.* The main reason Jesse Jackson achieved modest success in the Democratic primaries in 1984 and 1988 was *because* of his race. His appeal to blacks was *because* he was black. A white Jesse Jackson, so far to the political left, would go *nowhere* even in left-tilted Democratic primaries, and *nowhere fast* in a general election. This Cuomo act of pander became commonplace.

He came to believe that he was the adjudicator of who was "compassionate" and who wasn't in our compassionate society. In fact, the blue collar ethnics who had supported him in the past, abandoned him in droves in his 1994 re-election effort. For voicing concerns about the decline of their neighborhoods, and the size of the metastasizing welfare state, these law-abiding Americans were subtly branded as *ignoramuses* and *racists* by Mario.

I voted against King Cuomo in 94, when he was at long last thrown off the government payroll. He soon emerged as a talk radio show host, or pardon me, "thought radio show host," as he smugly referred to his program (since cancelled because it was a crashing bore). Arrogant as ever, he's spewing "compassion" in his patented mean-spirited style.

Compassion is more than a word, Mario. You might want to consider that before opening your yap!

<u>No Justice, No Pizza</u>

I helped put a drug-dealer back in business on the streets of the South Bronx.

Sorry about that.

It happened in the early 1990s. I was summoned to jury duty, and picked to serve. As a civic-minded citizen who always answered my call, I trekked to the Bronx County Court House on 161st Street and the Grand Concourse--in the shadow of Yankee Stadium.

The case seemed simple enough. Two undercover cops had staked out a location where a drug exchange took place. The team consisted of one cop on the stakeout and another nearby in a patrol car. When the purchase was made, the stakeout cop radioed his partner and the arrest was made at the scene. The drug dealer, named Calvin, was picked up on the spot with the "goods" on him. Open and shut case, I'd say.

But I was a liberal back then. And one of my favorite movies was, and is, *Twelve Angry Men*. Forgive me if I wanted to be Henry Fonda for a day.

The accused had a lackluster Legal Aid attorney. He stammered through a defense which claimed the cops had blundered by picking up the wrong guy. He showed a few snapshots of the scene as *Exhibit A*, hoping to implant reasonable doubt into our minds.

Calvin, the accused drug seller, was black. The make-up of the final Twelve on the jury consisted of two whites (myself and another guy), five blacks, and five Hispanics. All of us got to hold the drugs that were taken from Calvin. Vials of cocaine, bags of marijuana, etc., were passed around in the dealer's utilitarian valise. This was the prosecution's case. Saw Calvin make a sale, and nabbed him.

If we the jury were to free Calvin, we had to believe that the cops were either framing him, or picked up the wrong guy.

A stretch? Not for a Bronx jury. We took an initial vote to see where we stood. The five blacks and yours truly raised their hands to vote "Not Guilty." The five Hispanics and the other *colorless* person said "Guilty."

The deliberations are something of a fog

to me now. I remember we got a free lunch. We got to order from a local deli. We couldn't go outside, which meant that I had to forgo my usual slice of pizza. I recall *White Guy Number Two* angrily saying to me, "Are you buying this?" He was initially adamant that the evidence was clear cut in favor of conviction. The Hispanic jurors agreed with him.

The blacks and I weren't going to budge. Calvin was destined to go free.

Little by little our jury crumbled under the pressures of intimidation, apathy, and the ticking clock. Most of us serving just wanted to get out of our tiny "prison cell" of a deliberation room and go home. This dinky case with two witnesses took two weeks to complete. One day the judge had other business to attend to. Another day the Assistant DA was sick. Lunch breaks sometimes were four hours.

The last hold out for a guilty verdict was a gentleman who spoke only broken English. When asked by the exasperated Eleven how he could still possibly believe in the guilt of the accused, after our "rigorous" fact-finding debate, he said, in a heavily Spanish-accented English, *"Eee ad droogs on eem."* The man with the least capacity to express himself in English, summed up the case better than the rest of us. *He had drugs on him!*

Needless to say, even this last hold-out gave in. He wanted to go home, too.

God Does Make Junk

You call another human being trash!!!
- an angry Zeke, who has himself referred to
some men as "pieces of shit"
and some women as "cunts."

In December of 1984, a lanky, bespectacled nerd named Bernhard Geotz opened fire on a group of young thugs in a New York City subway car. Geotz, who had been mugged and robbed before, felt like "a cornered rat," he said, as the youths surrounded him and asked him for money. *Pow. Pow. Pow.* The rest is history. Geotz fled the scene and headed to *Live Free or Die* country, where he eventually turned himself in.

Before admitting he was the "guilty" party, New York papers branded him the "Subway Vigilante." Then Mayor Koch lectured city residents that vigilantism was *a no-no* and that he, in *no* uncertain terms, condemned such acts. (Koch was totally confused, and didn't know whose side to take for political advantage.)

It was now up to a grand jury to decide

whether or not Geotz actually committed a crime. Yours truly, a bleeding heart liberal who had just voted for Walter Mondale, participated in a mock debate for a fledgling video enthusiast. The topic of the debate was *Bernie Geotz: Victim or Victimizer.*

As the token liberal at this war of words, I condemned the "brutal, over-reaction" of the *Subway Gunman*, as Geotz was sometimes called. My neighbor-opponent matter-of-factly defended Geotz: "He was being robbed, fearing for his life, and he reacted accordingly. What would have happened to Bernie if he hadn't had the gun?"

My level-headed neighbor was speaking from the heart, not from some ideological bent. His heart bespoke the reality of traveling underground in a subway car. My pabulum defense of the wild bunch was *lip-service liberalism* at its worst.

The lesson to be learned from this experience: Beware of spouting-off in front of rolling cameras. For your pious platitudes might just end up on *America's Funniest Home Videos*. Spewers of leftist dribble be *especially* wary.

Fortunately, I have custody of the only copy of the *Bernie Geotz Debate*, and have no intention of turning it over. If *Hard Copy* offers me $50,000 for it, I might reconsider.

And now the rest of the story. Geotz was compelled to do eight months in prison for possession of an unregistered weapon (an unheard-of sentence for the crime). Grandstander supreme, lawyer William Kunstler, did his best to crucify Geotz and remove him from the streets of New York. When Geotz was diagnosed with testicular cancer after leaving prison, the always *compassionate* Kunstler said, "Maybe there is a God after all." Kunstler painted Geotz as a monster and the hoodlums as tragic victims of a racist and a racist society.

One of the choir boys on the subway that fateful night was a fellow named James Ramseur. With a history of criminal acts, Ramseur was put back out on the streets time and again.

This guy made the infamous Willie Horton, of Dukakis-furlough fame, look like Rodney Allen Rippy. *He was bad news.* While Kunstler wanted to cleanse society of the likes of Bernie Geotz, his client Jimmy Ramseur went on to rape and sodomize an eighteen-year-old pregnant girl.

Mollycoddling the Muggers

Give them jobs...
this will solve all our problems.
- Zeke

Addendum: Bill Kunstler died in 1995. His legacy is maintained by his protégé, Ron Kuby. Kuby won a 43 million dollar civil suit against Geotz on behalf of one of the muggers shot by him over ten years ago. In a *60 Minutes* commentary segment featuring a debate between columnists Molly Ivins and Stanley Crouch, the twosome debated the latest Geotz case.

Ivins chastised Geotz for not being *"wussy-but-wise"* and giving up his money, and lauded the jury for not buying his self-defense argument. Crouch put the 43 million dollar judgment in perspective when he said, "I don't believe someone should get workmen's comp just because he had a bad crime day."

Molly Ivins, columnist/amorphous blob, is out-of-touch with reality. Geotz is no hero, but he's paying a hefty price for minding his own business on that subway car that December day.

Start Spreading The News...

Do you come here often?

-- Senator Ted Kennedy,
to a Brooklyn soup kitchen patron

Because New York Has Tough Problems...

Rudy Giuliani

A Bronx Tale

*I won't be wronged, I won't be insulted,
and I won't be laid a hand on.
I don't do these things to others,
and I require the same from them.
- John Bernard Books played by John Wayne
in The Shootist*

In the summer of 1978, two friends and I went over to Fordham Road, a short ride from Kingsbridge on the Number 20 bus, to see a lame action-movie called *Hooper*, starring Burt Reynolds.

What is memorable about this particular excursion is a post-movie incident. Walking the couple of blocks from the Valentine Theater to the bus stop, proved to be a frightening experience for me and my two friends. We were *quasi-nerdy* youths, and the once safe and vibrant Fordham Road no longer had the Welcome Mat out for innocent teens.

Four street punks made this quite clear. One took off his belt and brandished it. We tried to be brave and not run, but we picked up our pace. Then one of the restless youths exclaimed, "Why don't we slice them up!" This tested our fleet-footedness. We ran. *(Molly Ivins would be proud.)*

Feeling cowardly for running, we nevertheless realized we had little choice. We weren't carrying knives, or toting guns, or schooled in the martial arts.

What I neglected to mention about this incident in the Bronx, was that a *bias crime* was committed. This was long before bias crime laws and the great *sensitivity* of the 1990s, however. The youngsters in question were Latinos and used *(God, it's almost too awful to repeat!)* the epithet **"White Boys"** on more than one occasion. Geez, that hurt more than the belt buckle!

Epilogue: *Hooper* didn't win an *Academy Award*. The youths in question probably whacked more people with their belts, and I daresay, they probably got to use their knives. One or more of these young men is likely a statistic.

How much compassion is in order here? Since Mario Cuomo's not available, I'll take a shot at it. These victims-of-society were preying on their victimizers--three popcorn-eating sixteen-year-olds coming home from a silly action movie. The victims didn't appear malnourished and they wore genuine leather belts.

Save your compassion for those who deserve it. I can't help but think the world would be an infinitesimally better place without the likes of such belters who most likely graduated to knives and/or guns.

I can hear the liberal pundits crying out in exasperation: "What do you want to do? Build more jails?"

Yes. Even Mr. C saw the wisdom in this.

<u>No More Mr. Nice Guy</u>

*The only thing we have to fear is fear itself--
nameless, unreasoning, unjustified terror
which paralyzes needed
efforts to convert retreat into advance.
-Franklin Delano Roosevelt*

*Ask not what your country can do for you--
ask what you can do for your country.
-John Fitzgerald Kennedy*

*Don't dis the sis.
-David Norman Dinkins*

In 1989, after a twelve-year reign of a sniping, dome-headed mayor, New Yorkers made history by electing their first *person of color* to that office.

Indeed, the incumbent Ed Koch had worn out his welcome. A municipal corruption scandal raged in his final years, so much so that the mayor in his book, *Citizen Koch*, said that he actually contemplated suicide. It was time to remove the *Sniper's Nest* from Gracie Mansion.

Suicidal thoughts notwithstanding, Koch didn't know how to bow out gracefully. He opted to run for a fourth term. (Term limits have since been passed in New York City, limiting a mayor to two four-year terms.)

This time though, Koch faced a serious opponent. David Dinkins, the Manhattan borough president, most famous for failing to file an income tax return for four consecutive years in the 1970s, was the presumptive favorite. He was an African-American, and considered an all-around good guy. It was time for New Yorkers to *get with the program.*

Still a practicing liberal in 1989, I voted for Dinkins in the Democratic primary. Koch's grating persona had become unbearable. And Dinkins seemed a reasonable enough alternative.

But on primary night, I already regretted my vote. For Dinkins, basking in his triumph, sounded an exclusionary note in his victory statement to supporters; a precursor of his looming, inept mayoralty.

Dinkins campaigned against Koch as a "healer," as a man capable of unifying the city. Koch, Dinkins claimed, was incapable of smothering the smoldering tensions between the races.

Running a fall campaign against a rare viable Republican, Rudy Giuliani, the Dinkins people, not-too-subtly, said a vote for Rudy was a vote for *intolerance.*

I voted for "intolerance."

"The healer" won. And for the next four years, the *Big Apple* was a tinderbox of racial tensions. A Hasidic scholar named Yankel Rosenbaum was "lynched" in Crown Heights, Brooklyn in 1991, amidst a riot, because the mayor of all New York refused to allow the police to crack down on the marauders. A New York Post headline blared **DAVE, DO SOMETHING.** Yet the mayor permitted the "unrest" to go virtually unchecked for over twenty-four hours, implying that it was best to let the people involved *pass some wind*. When a Korean grocery store was targeted by black protesters as a racist enterprise, they blocked the store's entrance. Once again, *the mayor of all the people* did not permit the police to do their job. *So much for the storekeeper's civil rights*. Mr. Dinkins, "the healer," had struck again. And then there was the illegal alien drug dealer who was shot by cops in upper Manhattan's notorious Washington Heights. Dinkins raced to the dead dealer's family to comfort them, sending the unmistakable signal that the police were the guilty party.

How will I ultimately remember the Dinkins mayoralty? When a handful of young black males got a little fresh with their female peers in city swimming pools, a trend seemed to be developing. Dinkins, the moral leader and "the healer," wasted no time in condemning the youthful miscreants. "Don't dis the sis," he offered.

Thanks, David, for your inspiring leadership and heartfelt words. Your contribution to the liberal bedrock has been overwhelming.

Whine and Spectator Radio

From my vantage point, the biggest political bozo on the scene is a former mayor with a radio program. His name is Ed Koch. (Mario Cuomo is in a class by himself.)

Koch epitomizes some of the worst aspects of the career politician. He's not corrupt *per se*, but he craves attention in his every waking hour. He's got to be in the spotlight. He has an insatiable need to be heard. When he lost his bid for a fourth term for mayor, Koch gravitated to television and radio stations, signing on as an all-knowing pundit. He got weekly newspaper and syndicated movie review columns. He's even gone commercial, shilling for such diverse products as *Dunkin' Donuts*, *Snapple Iced Tea* and *H.I.P. of New York*, an over-priced HMO with a dubious history.

Listening to his radio show on New York's *WABC* is an endurance test. He starts each program by proclaiming, "Here I am, your *Voice of Reason*." He has cleverly labeled himself a "liberal with sanity."

I beg to differ. When a caller phones his program to disagree with him, he shrieks, "Stop!" And the caller can only continue if he admits to having had his mind changed by a stream of *Koch logic.*

The former mayor demands obsequiousness from all who phone in, and he's positively aglow when someone tells him that he was a "great mayor."

He wasn't.

Koch endorsed Rudy Giuliani for mayor against the incumbent David Dinkins in 1993. His support was considered a big factor in putting Giuliani over the top.

Soon after Rudy took office, however, and started accomplishing things Koch only dreamed about (like merging the transit and housing cops with the NYPD, coupled with record drops in crime), the former mayor became his biggest critic, going so far as to call Giuliani "meshugana" (a Yiddish word meaning "crazy").

Besides policy differences, Koch didn't like the way Giuliani treated people, he said. He called Giuliani a "bad guy" and "bully."

It's fair to say that Koch has a point. Giuliani's a control freak, browbeater, and all around mean guy. *But, for Ed Koch to make this accusation....*

Koch wrote two books of memoirs (*Mayor* and *Politics*) while a sitting mayor, in which he spoke openly about the failings of some of the fellow pols he was working with in city government. He once made New York City council president Carol Bellamy cry, he wrote. (She wasn't up to playing with *the big boys!*) His cunning and knowledge made the unprepared Congressman Charlie Rangel sweat.

And this insulting style was his *modus operandi* throughout his twelve years in office. It's okay, I guess, for him to say Giuliani has behaved like a "horse's ass." This isn't meant to be personal, or isn't "vul-gah," to quote the former mayor.

Ed Koch is *clueless in Manhattan*. Politicians are often removed from the everyday living of the men and women they represent.

Yet Koch fancies himself an authority on New York City and its neighborhoods. He will deny that the city has declined dramatically in the last twenty-five years, the direct result of white flight to suburbia. *The Ice People Goeth.*

Why has this happened? Why are so many formerly hospitable neighborhoods *user-unfriendly* today? Too much immigration, both legal and illegal, in the last three decades has driven down the city's quality of life. There are more illegal immigrants in the *Big Apple* than there are people in the state of Wyoming! The school system is over-crowded, violent, and schizophrenic. (115 languages being spoken there at last count.)

Ed Koch is a devotee of today's nonsensical immigration laws. When the late Congresswoman Barbara Jordan's presidential commission on immigration reported its findings and recommendations--a 30% cut in the number of legal immigrants admitted to this country each year--Koch cried that she should be "denounced!" for advising so.

Why? Only *The Voice of Reason* knows. He's always quick to cite the will of the American people when it suits him. ("80% of the people want the minimum wage increased!") When it's not in his interest, like on the immigration question, he conveniently fails to cite overwhelming public support.

Then there's Koch's one-man polling operation. He has said on his radio show that "at least 25% of the American people are bigots." How has he arrived at this conclusion? If a caller to his show cites a fact that is not verifiable and not on his personal agenda, the ex-mayor will jump all over him.

Ed Koch is knowledgeable in the text book sense of a crafty politician. But the reality is that he, like so many politicians near you, lives on *Fantasy Island.* They make our laws, many of them in anonymity, and are grossly out of touch.

So why do we elect these people? In Koch's case, it was his schtick--he was entertaining. And like so many successful politicians, he knew which hot-button issues to press. President Clinton, master politician, knew that demagoguing the minor reforms Republicans proposed in Medicare and Social Security, was a winner politically.

Ed Koch's oft-repeated question to the citizenry in New York (and everywhere else he goes) is "How'm I doin'?"

You *don't* really want to know, Mr. Mayor.

The Passing of the Bars

*Have you survived a suicide attempt
made on public property?
Has a bartender sold you a drink which led to
your involvement in
a fatal hit-and-run accident?
- questions asked by Barry Green of the
Green & Fazio law offices on a
Saturday Night Live skit.*

Throughout the 1990s, in New York City parks everywhere, the bars are coming out. For you prohibitionists: Hold off the celebration. We're talking simian, not inebriate.

Monkey bars are being systematically removed from all the parks because a few accidents have occurred in the past century. Kids love monkey bars. And playing on something that requires climbing can get a kid hurt. But kids in little leagues can get hurt. And so can kids in swimming pools....

What's then the real reason for the banning of the bars? *Lawsuits.* The city has been sued on more than one occasion when a child fell and hit his head, or broke some limb, while cavorting on the monkey bars.

We can thank the sordid legal profession and the current litigious climate for this outrage against kids at play. *1-800-LAWYER* commercials pollute the air twenty-four hours a day, soliciting "victims" of accidents.

Apparently the old adage--*accidents can happen*--no longer applies. Parental responsibility of an honest mishap, without running to some firm full of leeches, is becoming as outdated as the typewriter.

The Democratic party's special allegiance to the trial lawyers of America and their unscrupulous lobby, is a pact with the devil.

Greece Is The Word

One of the benefits of living in New York City is the superabundance of Greek diners that dot the five boroughs.

I frequent the rarest of birds in the Greek diner pantheon--a place run by Greeks with charisma, instead of the more common *cipher-owner.* And to add to this luck of the draw, my diner serves the world's greatest hamburgers, uniquely seasoned and served with *a winning smile.*

This story is heading for a smoke-filled room. Now, I detest cigarette smoke and am often amazed at the obliviousness of smokers to the world around them. Certainly they have the right to smoke, but not to send their second-hand remains in the direction of those who choose not to partake in their cancer-causing habit.

This said, I'm dismayed at some of the anti-smoking legislation being passed. I'm glad that smoking the noxious weed in public buildings has been barred.

It's the private sector that concerns me. New York City passed a law outlawing smoking in restaurants/diners with seating capacity of more than thirty-five. The day after the law took effect, I visited my favorite little Greek diner. I surmised that their cozy little size put them perilously close to having to comply with the **NO SMOKING** decree.

Noting two chairs missing from a couple of tables in the back of the place, I decided to count the stools at the counter and seating capacity at the tables and booths. I came up with thirty-four.

The missing chairs made the diner legally a *smoker's haven*. While I'd prefer no smoking on the premises, I voluntarily dine at this unique *greasy spoon*, smoke and all, because the food and the folk transcend the smoke.

There are some places I will not frequent because the air quality is worse than Los Angeles on ozone alert. But let the owners of these establishments decide whether they want their businesses to be smoke-free or -filled. Then you and I, as consumers, can choose whether to patronize them.

Government, butt out.

Quote The Raving

Outside of the killings, we have one
of the lowest crime rates
in the country.

--Washington, DC Mayor
Marion Barry, 1989

ICATESSEN
Coca-Cola
SAMS PIZZA
Dale FLORIST
WE DELIVER
TEL. 796-8281

The Not Necessarily Top Ten Stream of Consciousness Reasons Why I'm No Longer A Liberal

1. This **Mario Cuomo** letter to the *New York Daily News* after the O.J. Simpson verdict:

    Manhattan: Most whites believe O.J. Simpson is guilty and are stunned. Most blacks are pleased, although it's not clear to me that they actually believe O.J. didn't do it. But race was not the decisive factor. In truth, whites are ignoring the rules that control the courtroom. Blacks are cheering the jury for putting the law first.

    Mark Fuhrman, the lack of direct evidence and other reservations add up to "reasonable doubt." A more professional prosecution might have produced a different result, but the prosecution botched it by using racist Fuhrman. The jury played by the rules, but the great majority of whites would have preferred that it ignore them. Now that's really dangerous.

    Mario Cuomo

Lack of *Direct Evidence?* Mario, the beaning that ended your professional baseball career is finally taking its toll *big-time*.

2. **Ted Kennedy.** Don Imus has called the Massachusetts Senator a "fat slob with a head the size of a dumpster."

He's looking better today, and I'm happy for him. But it's high time the Democratic party got over its infatuation with the Kennedys. This past Democratic convention saw old standard-bearers shunted aside, while the Kennedy family was featured prominently. *Jimmy Carter, where are you?*

3. **Morley Safer** points the bony finger of indignation at the people of Wausau, Wisconsin. It seems the *60 Minutes* star saw something diabolical about the lifelong residents of this town trying to stem the massive influx of Vietnamese Muong people into their neighborhoods. People who were swelling the welfare rolls, having more children than they could afford, dramatically increasing the crime rate, and crowding the schools with non-English speaking boys and girls. Morley intoned to an activist town resident, who was pushing various proposals to do something about the immigration debacle, "This sounds like something else."

Safer, a celebrity and multi-millionaire,

living in a mega-bucks door-manned high-rise in Manhattan (where, trust me, the city doesn't plop welfare families), passing judgment on the people of Wausau. Hmmm....

4.   **Menace 2 Society**. *WCBS-TV* in New York has a local news program that once upon a time was called *Channel 2 News.* To make it appear more hip and 1990s, some advertising whiz advised a name change. Now it's called *2 News.* Anyway, when a proposal in Suffolk County on Long Island arose to make English its official language, *2 News* reported the story from its patented professional angle. A reporter opened a segment with a taped piece of the immigrant groups that would be affected by the law if it was passed. She said, "They come from Ireland, Poland, and Russia...all trying to find a piece of the American dream."

I've conducted a little survey among my friends of Irish-background and their relatives. And you know what? I haven't found *one* of them who knew even a distant kinsman, going back generations, who didn't speak English. As for the Poles and Russians, like most Europeans, they often have a working knowledge of English, and if they don't, are willing to learn.

How come *2 News* didn't know this?

5. **Simonizing America.** I like former presidential candidate and Senator from Illinois, Paul Simon. He seems like a decent, honest man. Nevertheless, he embodied the self-serving liberal when he was asked in a 1988 Democratic presidential primary debate which former presidents' portraits he'd hang in the cabinet room if he was elected president. It was a fluff question to be sure, but it was an opportunity to get a little insight into the candidate's character. Simon said, "The cabinet room is a working room...I'd hang a picture of a steel worker...a single mother...."

Get the picture?

6. **Mourning in America.** If we had a parliamentary system of government with a head of state as well as government, Bill Clinton would be ideal in the state role. He'd make a great head of state, delivering heartfelt eulogies and affecting a superb mourning face. Commerce Secretary Ron Brown's death opened my eyes real wide. I never realized what a great, inspirational man he was.

I thought he was an ambitious party flack under a dark cloud, who faced a criminal indictment.

7. **My nephew.** In grades one through three he got to go to the school in his suburban neigh-

borhood. It was less than a ten-minute ride. Courtesy of a some all-knowing bureaucrats, his school was certified as improperly balanced. My eight-year-old nephew would now have to go across town. And this would require an hour-and-a-half bus ride with umpteen stops. *Each way!*

This might sound radical, but shouldn't parents who pay the property taxes to support the schools have some say in these matters?

8. **Flag stealing.** In my tiny front alcove below sea level, I placed an American flag in a flower pot. Through the years my neighbors have had flower pots stolen, and sometimes just the flowers. Halloween pumpkins have been swiped, along with Christmas ornaments. Now my flag.

Old Glory is one item that fewer and fewer of the new breed in the Bronx seem to want, so I was kind of surprised.

9. **Good questions.**
"The big question the American people have to ask their politicians is--what's your plan? If the politician is voting to keep the status quo, keep these numbers of immigrants coming, what is their plan for handling 130 million more people over the next half century? The fact is nobody

has a plan."
- Roy Beck, author of
Re-Charting America's Future

10. **A Speck of a man.** Mass murderer Richard Speck was the subject of an *Investigative Reports* with Bill Kurtis. It seems that the murderer of nine young women in a single night was somehow able to make a pornographic videotape while behind bars in a *maximum security prison*. Somehow, too, this beast had grown breasts and had access to drugs and money. When asked in this clandestine video why he killed all those women, he said, "It wasn't their night." He added at one point that if the authorities knew how much fun he was having behind bars, they'd release him. To add insult-to-injury, because his death sentence had been commuted, he became eligible for parole after serving only seven years. This travesty forced the families of the victims to attend parole hearings year-after-year and beg that Speck not go free.

He didn't, and he had the time of his life.

PS: Before his trial, Speck tried to commit suicide and was saved by a team of dedicated doctors. He was then put on a suicide watch. It's time we ended the notion of the *suicide watch* for murderous swine.

Let them do it!

Miscellaneous Musings

...and Tyler, Too. I had a music teacher in high school, a very nice man, who was the father of rock star, Steve Tyler, head of the band, *Aerosmith.* Tyler's dad was proud of his son, and one day passed around his photo. "This is my son, Steve," he said. A quipping classmate, known for her sassiness, summed up the general consensus when she saw the picture. *"Uuuuggh,"* she said. If you know what *Aerosmith's* Tyler looks like, you'll understand where she was coming from. If you listen to their music, you'll understand more fully America's cultural demise. I sometimes think I'm in a parallel dimension, because I can't fathom why anybody would voluntarily pump such grinding sound into his ear.

Life Behind Bars. I live behind bars. It's a 90s thing. How come so many of us have to put bars on our doors and windows, where twenty years ago it was unheard of? To paraphrase Captain Kirk, "Explain!"

Hanz and Franz, Americans? Which foreign country has provided us with the most immigrants? Few people whom I polled answered correctly. *Surprise.* Germany leads the pact with 11.7% (over seven million) of the total US immigrants entering the country between 1820-1993. Italy is next with 8.9% (about four-and-a-half million). The reason for the confusion begs the question: Where have all the German-Americans gone? From grammar school through high school, us kids were conscious of our ancestry. Italian, Irish...but no German. New York City, at the turn-of-the century, was chock-full of German neighborhoods. Today, even *Germantown* in Manhattan has vanished. Where have all their descendants gone? Clearly, they've assimilated so fully into the broader America and are no longer part of a hyphenated America.

This is the *ultimate* immigrant story.

Death Be Not Proud. During millionaire publisher Steve Forbes' campaign for president, I was impressed with his upbeat demeanor. He seemed down-to-earth for a guy worth almost half a billion dollars. Oh, he sniped with the best of them, and took a few cheap shots along the way, but he rarely displayed real anger. Then one day a reporter asked him a question about Dr. Jack Kevorkian's acquittal in his latest assisted suicide trial. Forbes' *deer-in-headlights* look assumed a Clint Eastwood toughness. "I think he's a murderer who should be put away for life," he answered. I was shocked by the venom in his voice. I *like* Jack Kevorkian. I *like* what he does. Sure, he's a bit ghoulish. *So what!* I can't fathom how anyone could pass judgment on a terminally ill person, in perpetual pain, wanting out of his living nightmare. *Keep it up, Dr. K.* And, as for the unbiased press, I've heard Kevorkian repeatedly referred to as *"Dr. Death"* and the *"Angel of Death."*

Pejorative labels?

I Wonder
As I Wander

It is easier to love humanity as a whole than to love one's neighbor.

--Eric Hoffer

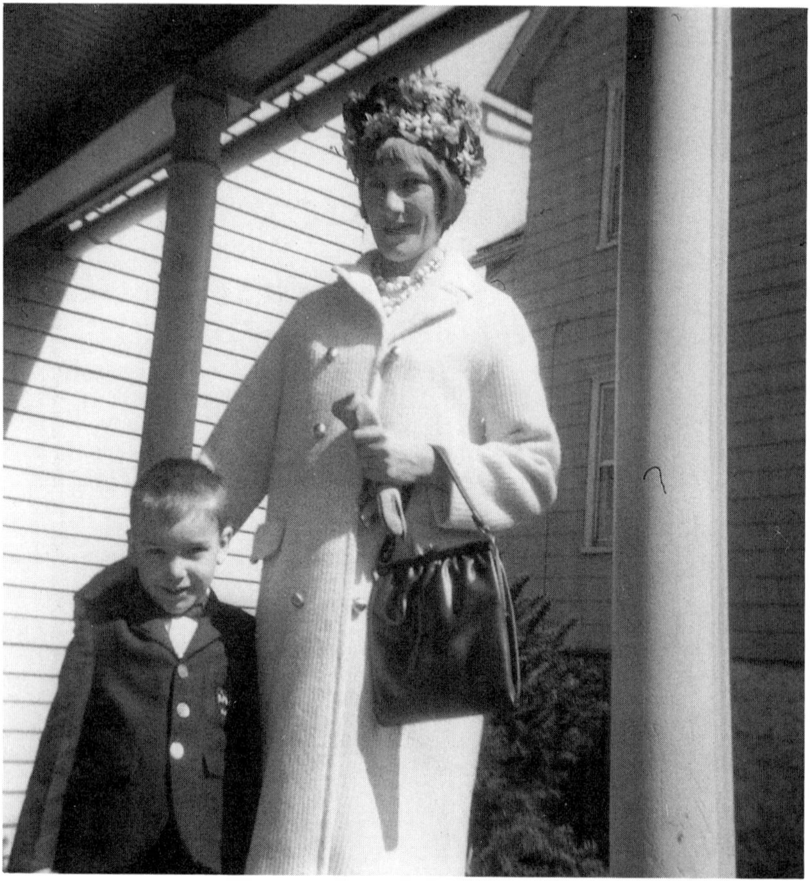

The Wonder Years

I am a by-product of Catholic education from grade one through college. I can only count kindergarten as a public school experience.

St. John's grammar school was a few blocks from home. It was never debated in the Nigro house, and most Catholic families in the neighborhood, that parochial school was the way to go. Back in the 60s and 70s it was affordable, even for families with modest means. My father's four-to-midnight shift at the General Post Office at Penn Station put five Nigros through Catholic school. (Mom ultimately got a part-time job.)

It couldn't happen today. I attended Cardinal Spellman High School in the East Bronx when tuition was $800 per school year. Now it's over $3000. To the media and political elitists, who think they know what's best for us-- the ones who oppose tax relief for parents who choose to send their kids to private or parochial schools--I say, *give 'em a break.* New York City public schools personify the reality of the 1990s--guns and clutter are the rule and the English language is far from sacrosanct. The "choice" for many parents living in the world's most renowned city is no *choice* at all. *Leave.*

PS: Even with my extensive Catholic education--and I'm glad that I went to the schools that I did--I don't go to mass on Sundays and haven't since high school. I am a *hatch 'em, match 'em, and dispatch 'em* church goer these days: baptisms, weddings, and funerals.

A Garbage Bag For Jesus?

I'll admit to committing blasphemy from time-to-time, and not having the highest regard for organized religion and dogma.

Still, I was taken aback by a decision made by a New York City public school, involving a plastic garbage bag.

Here's the story. My grammar school alma mater, St. John's, has shrunk dramatically in enrollment since I graduated in 1976. Correspondingly, its sister public school, P.S. 7 has swelled--indicative of changing neighborhood demographics.

St. John's diminished student population enabled the New York Archdiocese to lease one of its two school buildings. Atop each of the St. John's buildings is, you guessed it, a cross. A modest stone cross.

In the 1990s, where separation of church and state have been taken to new heights, a big time dilemma confronted the Archdiocese and the city's Board of Education. When the new tenant took control of the former Catholic school, the cross remained. Since the building was only being leased, the cross wasn't about to be destroyed, as many bureaucrats desired. Their solution--cover the cross, the most sacred symbol in Christianity, with a super-sized *Hefty* bag, and place a Public School Number 7 banner beneath it.

There was some murmuring in the community, about how this was a slap in the face of Catholics, but nothing was done about it.

After all, the damage to a child's attending P.S. 7 and seeing a cross on the premises, might be irreparable to his young psyche.

I don't favor religious markers in the public schools, but I can't help but feel covering part of the building with a trash bag is yet another zany example of the lengths the *ACLU* bunch will go.

An educated kid might just be a little curious, and ask, "What's in the bag?"

"Oh, just a cross."

"Why is it in the bag?"

Why indeed.

The Hell With Original Sin

Although a born and raised Catholic, I never bought, even as a boy, the concept of *original sin*. We were taught that if a newborn infant died before his baptism, he would be relegated to an eternity in *Limbo*, and not be granted passage through the *Pearly Gates*. *Limbo* is thought to be a bland in-between, for those without the necessary credentials to get into Heaven, but not sufficiently evil to burn in the fires of Hell.

The notion of *Limbo* is absurd. And overpopulating it with cooing and wailing infants is even more ridiculous. The most innocent of human beings are *obviously* the newborn. Still, Church teaching put out this *Limbo* line.

I also don't believe in original sin for us *"Euro"* Americans. I wasn't born with a smudge on my soul because, many generations ago, some plantation owners, with the same pigmentation as mine, owned slaves or gave chicken pox to some Indians.

There was this obscure governor from an obscure state named Bill Clinton. He was, for some inexplicable reason, the Democratic party front-runner for president in 1992. As a Democrat, with waning enthusiasm, I went on a search for a candidate I could support. I found Jerry Brown.

I didn't think he could win, but I liked his maverick platform and anti-establishment histrionics. He lambasted the monied interests in politics, and blasted the shallow media who insisted on covering presidential politics like the old *Beat The Clock* game show. When he got into a verbal scrape with *NBC*'s Tom Brokaw during a debate, Brown looked the part of the ideal protest candidate.

He told Brokaw, who wanted to keep him from giving out his oft-repeated 800 number, that he wasn't going to permit a member of the media establishment to tell him what he could, or could not say, in a free debate. The anchor *fumed* at Brown's insolence. *I loved it!*

The problem with Jerry Brown was that he was reinventing himself again. He wasn't supposed to become Clinton's Number One opponent. When he did, he devolved into a panderer extraordinaire, donning a *UAW* jacket in Detroit and scaring seniors in Pensecola.

Being a *Brown-ee*, I was offered the opportunity to become a Brown delegate to the Democratic National Convention in New York. A form was mailed to me with a *"Who Am I?"* survey. I had the option to check off one of these groups: African-American, Latino, Native American, and Asian-Pacific American.

Wasn't somebody missing here? Gee, not even a *Euro*-American....

It was bad enough having to check-off the group to which I belonged--but I wasn't even given one. It was a classic 1990s Democratic party maneuver. If Brown, playing the insurgent for 1992, couldn't cut out this bifurcating crap, than who could?

By the time the New York primary rolled around in April, I held my nose and voted for him. By then I was thoroughly disgusted with the flake who, months earlier, I had sent the campaign maximum of $100 to his *We The People* effort. To add insult-to-injury, Brown was now promising to tap Jesse Jackson as his running mate.

I Know Why The Bird Cage Is Messy

Beware of Greeks bearing gifts, colored men looking for loans, and whites who understand the negro.

--Adam Clayton Powell, Jr.

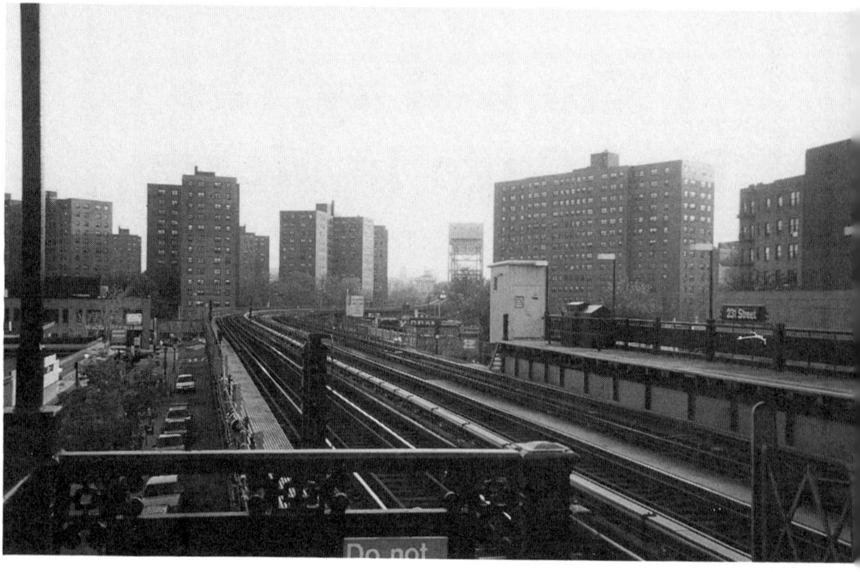
231 Street
Do not

You Were Somebody

*The reality is that there are more white people
in poverty than black people.
White people commit more crimes
and suffer more arrests.
More white families go without
health care, rely on food stamps,
are forced on unemployment or welfare.
More white children go to public schools
starved for resources,
unable to give their kids a fair start.
- from a Jesse Jackson Op-Ed column*

I was impressed with Jesse Jackson when he ran for president in 1984 and 1988. Of course, I was more inclined then to buy into his leftist social and economic agenda.

I found Jackson to be both intelligent and charismatic. But as the years have passed, and the legal civil rights' battles became fewer, Jackson has become a ridiculous anachronism and caricature.

Today, as he fishes around for boycott and protest opportunities, Jesse has exposed himself as a mega-publicity hound and little else. His *Academy Award* protest, replete with rainbow-colored ribbons, was vintage *Jesse Jackson Today.*

The man is obviously feeling the pains of rejection. Louis Farrakhan gets all the press talking about space aliens and mad scientists. So, Jesse's got to make his own news by staging demonstrations at gas stations, juice bars, supermarkets, and car washes.

Jackson, still an intransigent defender of Affirmative Action laws great and small, is always quick to point out that there are more whites than blacks on welfare--more whites than blacks below the poverty line. *True enough, Jesse.* But why not carry this reality a step further?

You, Jesse Jackson, believe in discrimination against one group of poor people because of the color (or lack of it) of their skin. Isn't that true? Affirmative Action does not seek to help the white folk on the bottom of the economic ladder.

Jesse, I've heard you claim that it's a misnomer to suggest that quotas and set-asides hurt some people. *Explain* how this works? *Explain* how one group of people can be favored over another, based solely on race, and nobody loses?

You've got a lot of *explaining* to do, Jesse.

Affirmative Action, 2020

Coming attractions: Affirmative Action programs for the children and grandchildren of *White Trash* and other persons of non-color who were discriminated against in the latter part of the 20th century by a host of federal and state laws.

**Everything Is Racial...
In Its Own Way**

The name Senator Joe McCarthy is synonymous with the excesses and intolerance of an era when the brand of communist or communist-sympathizer could destroy your life. There was a *Red Scare* in the 1950s, and it was the ultra-right who were the guilty parties.

It's in the history books now, and there aren't too many Americans who'd admit these days to being *pink down to their underwear.* In its place, and more pervasive and threatening to liberty, is the *Racist Scare* of the 1990s, the main by-product of the insidious world of political correctness.

In the 1990s, being branded a "racist" is akin to the 1950s "Red" smear. When McCarthy accused card-carrying American liberals of being communist dupes, it was overkill. He died a broken man, drowned in his crapulence.

Today, be careful what you say. If you want immigration reform, you're a racist. If you oppose Affirmative Action--no doubt about it--you want to hold minorities down, *you swine.* If you enumerate the deleterious effects of welfare, you're a bigot for sure.

This is the climate we live in. The Left represents the biggest threat to liberty in America. It's not Pat Robertson curing someone of a urinary tract infection through the television screen on *The 700 Club.* It's deviant lefties in positions of influence and power--in universities, courts, politics, and the media.

Congressman Charlie Rangel has taken the racist slur to new and absurd heights. He calls tax cuts "racist code words." *Got that?* If you favor lower taxes, you are no better than cosmeticized Klansman, David Duke.

**<u>Kweisi Mfume
Is A Silly Name...
And So Many Silly Things
Keep Happening</u>**

As you've read, I occasionally listen to Ed Koch's radio program. One morning on his show, the former mayor was talking about Congressman Kweisi Mfume (now *NAACP* president). He was pronouncing the man's last name with an unusual emphasis: *"M-fooom."* This got the goat of a listener who called Koch and told him that he was deliberately mispronouncing Mfume's name. He said this was "racist."

Koch denied the accusation. I don't think *The Bald One* was telling the truth. He was getting a kick out of saying a funny surname. Not too many Americans begin their names with two consonants.

In this age of hyper-sensitivity, having a few laughs with a person's name is tantamount to burning a cross on their front lawn.

Recently my eight-year-old nephew received a laudatory letter from one of his teachers. The man's name was Mr. Hoops. His brother, four years his junior, immediately sensed something humorous about it. "Mr. Poops," he said with a sly grin. His mother chastised him, but he sensed he could get away with saying it one more time and he did. "Mr. Poops," he said with a satisfied smirk.

I don't know if Mr. Hoops is black or white, but I can say without hesitation that my four-year-old nephew was not engaged in bigoted name-calling.

What Is This Thing Called Sin?

To let politics become a cesspool, and then avoid it because it is a cesspool, is a double crime.

--Howard Crosby

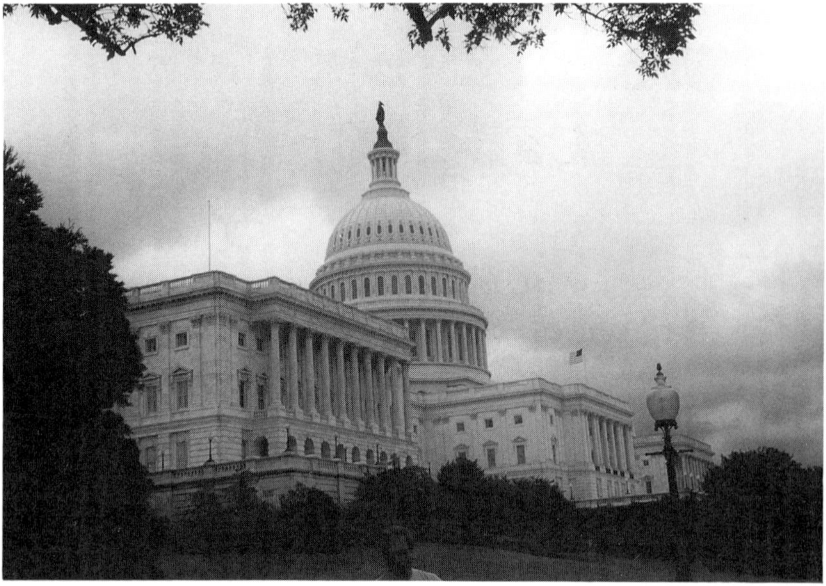

One Briefs Shining Moment

During the 1992 presidential campaign, candidate Bill Clinton told an audience of *MTVers* that he preferred wearing briefs to boxers. This revelation should have clued us in.

I'll be brief: A future President of the United States, chatting with the future of America, revealed the future. *Revealed indeed.* Candidate Clinton diminished the aura of the Presidency, by answering such a question. And knowing his propensity to prevaricate, he might have even been fibbing. The truth might be that he wears *Hanes Her Way.* Who knows?

The rest is history. To Washington came a Clinton White House, replete with characters like former bar bouncer, Craig Livingstone, with pivotal personnel and security powers. This man, who wasn't fit to work for *Sears* (courtesy of a routine background check), was "qualified" to hold a position of influence in the Clinton White House....

In 1992, George Bush was *persona non grata* in the hearts and minds of a majority of Americans, including me. But he was a decent guy. There was very little Maine to California enmity for George Bush. The prevailing feeling was: Let's retire this guy to Kennebunkport because he's "out of touch." Contrarily, most of Clinton's detractors have a profound distaste for the man and his bride.

Why the re-election then? Bill Clinton, by the economic standards of our time, deserved to be re-elected. Listening to Dole-Kemp blasting Clinton's record on the economy rang hollow. By historical standards the unemployment rate was low. Inflation was almost non-existent. (These days it always is in government figures, but never in supermarkets.) Interest rates were in the acceptable range (for those not paying them). And the federal deficit was declining.

Clinton did raise taxes, but Bob Dole's legislative history as an accomplice in numerous past *revenue enhancements* made him a discredited messenger of tax cuts. And the revolutionary changes he talked about in downsizing the IRS and simplifying the ridiculous tax code, he didn't seem to really mean.

Still, I voted for Dole-Kemp because I believe the Democratic party no longer represents the *Average Joe*; it's a party dominated by elitists and status quo flacks, catering to trial lawyers and big labor scumbags.

I see the economy, like life, as always running in cycles. When Clinton was first elected in 1992, the economy (the chief issue in the race against Bush) was statistically already on the rebound.

It's leadership issues that matter most to me. Virile challengers to the President could have grasped these; the Dole-Kemp team ran away from them. Case-in-point, the *California Civil Rights Initiative* (CCRI), which hopefully will outlaw race-based quotas in the state, was supported in the Republic platform. In today's political climate, ending Affirmative Action is supported overwhelmingly by the people, but condemned by the political, academic, and media elites. Politicians who dare denounce the discrimination of Affirmative Action, are tarred as...*need I say it?* Dole-Kemp were consummate *cowards* on this issue.

On the immigration issue, the twosome acquitted themselves no better. Kemp couched all his remarks against illegal immigration with caveats. "We want to stop illegal immigration," he said, "to protect legal immigration." When politicians can't take a stand against *illegal* immigration, without apologizing, we're in trouble.

I can no longer expect the Democratic party to forthrightly deal with any truly hot-button issues. So I sought some solace in the Republican party in 96, supporting Lamar Alexander in the primaries. (I thought then that he was the most viable candidate to run against Clinton and win, and still do.) After the Dole nomination, I looked to Governor Lamm and the Reform party. But the little weasel with the big ears and bucks made sure that didn't happen. (I never believed Lamm could get elected, and I usually don't make protest votes, but the former governor of Colorado would have been such a breath of fresh air, I'd have had to sign on.)

All this having been said: A Dole administration would have been a vast improvement over the current one based on this fact alone-- Bob and Liddy Dole are not Bill and Hillary Clinton.

I'm Not a Friend of Bill C

Thirty years ago, Clinton's behavior would have been absolutely disqualifying. Since the 1992 election, the public has learned far more about what is known, euphemistically, as the "character issue." Yet none of this appears to affect Clinton's popularity. It is difficult not to conclude that something about our moral perceptions and reactions has changed profoundly. If that change is permanent, the implication for our future is bleak. -from Slouching Towards Gomorrah by Robert H. Bork

As previously noted, I voted for Bill Clinton in 1992. Having cast my lot with Jerry Brown in the New York Primary, I reluctantly settled for the candidate whom I thought most "felt my pain."

My other options were the lackluster incumbent George Bush, or a cantankerous, paranoid millionaire. I found Bush to be a shameless panderer. Against Dukakis, he talked up the *Pledge of Allegiance* in flag factories. Running for re-election he seemed as equally facile and devoid of a rationale for wanting four more years in the White House.

Looking back on the pandering of George Bush, I have to concede that it doesn't compare to his successor's. George Bush's flip-flopping, and often self-serving campaign appearances were positively innocuous when up against Bill Clinton's shiftiness.

When I saw George and Barbara Bush making the interview rounds recently, talking about *Operation Desert Storm*, I couldn't help but respect his role as Commander-in-Chief. There was no *campaign-mode* Bush hyperventilating in the interviews. No bizarre non-sequiturs. A decent quality shined through.

Bill Clinton deserves no such respect. This is a man who was talking about *"maintaining (his) political viability"* when in college, trying to avoid the draft. I've got no problem with his endeavoring to evade a trip to Vietnam. But to be thinking about a cushy political career when thousands of his peers were dying....

Bill and Hillary Clinton epitomize the worst aspects of baby boomer hypocrisy. There is little that commends them as human beings. Clinton, insatiable libido and all, marries the equally ambitious Hillary in what has obviously been an arranged, open marriage.

What it all adds up to, when you wade through the Whitewaters and all the other sediment in their backgrounds, is a *trust-vacuum.*

It's disturbing to think that the *majority* of Clinton voters believe that the President is dishonest. We wouldn't want our supermarket bag-boy to be a liar and a cheat.

It's only the Presidency....

It Takes a Village Idiot...
To Respect Hillary Rodham

Like Rudolph, the Red-Nosed Reindeer, she'll go down in history. I'm talking about Hillary Rodham Clinton.

The feminist movement, and Sam Donaldson, would have us believe that Hillary's bad press is the by-product of a male-dominated society, jealous of all "strong" women. *Bess Truman be damned.*

Hillary Rodham is a "strong" woman all right. Her abundant ambition got her into the White House and involved in serious policy-making. And not a soul had ever cast a ballot for her.

Even if we trivialize Whitewater and her remarkable ability in locating fine investment opportunities, we still stumble on an unpleasant, vulgar, mean-spirited hypocrite. *And I say that with all due respect.*

This *Child of the 60s*, on her high horse, rides an equally ambitious moral cipher to the height of prestige and power--in the world! *Pretty remarkable story!*

What most sticks in my craw about Hillary Rodham is that she's no *Hillary Brooke.* Not even close. Hillary Rodham has wallowed for far too long in a counter-culture *noblesse oblige.* She has treated her help like crap.

Hillary has assumed a Queen-like posture and throws tantrums when her every whim isn't satisfied. She doesn't give a damn about anybody but herself. Ask the White House Travel Office personnel. Ask them when Hillary Rodham is out giving a speech about the plight of the abused and exploited American laborer.

Having worked in a retail environment for many years, I always did my best to please the customer *(well, usually).* So, I'm admittedly sensitive to help being maltreated. I've experienced the condescending attitudes of some customers, and I didn't like it. I didn't appreciate being looked upon as their servant.

Hillary Rodham considers herself a devoted liberal, concerned about the lower echelons of society and their plight. Well, Hillary, you're no Eleanor Roosevelt. Try Leona Helmsley. And you can talk to her in living color, without the assistance of a medium. But, hurry....

Clinton's No-Brainer

Zeke again. The subject matter: *Abortion.* Zeke, of course, is pro-choice, and so am I. As far as I'm concerned, I'd just as soon a woman have an abortion than a child she does not want and might abuse.

Where Zeke and I differ is another example of liberal excess. Abortion is a rather cruel affair. It's a woman's choice to make, but I wish it was removed from politics. An insane amount of theatrics, on both sides of the political aisle, are going on as I write these words.

Zeke, the father of two young daughters, once chastised me for suggesting that I saw nothing wrong with *parental notification* when minors seek abortions.

Logically, I asked him if he would want to know if one of his daughters *(God forbid!)* was having an abortion.

Zeke said, "*Nah*...wouldn't want to know."

I didn't believe him.

The Left-wing, with Zeke parroting their extreme position, has made the abortion issue one-dimensional. Abortion's the law of the land. But to sanitize it and all its ramifications is unrealistic and cold.

Can't a reasonable man be pro-choice, but codify his position by saying, "Hey, at twenty-four weeks, the fetus can live outside the womb...why not outlaw elective abortions after that period of time?"

If a politician takes this position, he is condemned by abortion-issue enthusiasts on both sides. The *Christian Coalition* and the feminist lobby are aghast at such pols' wishy-washy stances.

President Clinton shamelessly pandered to the ultra-abortion rights gang when he vetoed a ban on a procedure for partial-birth abortions. When a rational being looks at this technique, the conclusion can only be that it's infantacide. A baby, with his little fingers clasping and unclasping, and feet kicking, *has its brains sucked out of its head.*

I believe the mother's life comes first. But apparently these procedures aren't so nobly-inspired. Kate Michelman of the *National Abortion Rights Action League* says, "There is no such thing as a "partial birth."

Yes, Kate, there is a "partial birth."

Tomorrow Isn't Yesterday

Rowland Evans: "Should babies, children of illegal immigrants, be serviced by the American taxpayer?"

LA Mayor Richard Riordan: "Absolutely!"

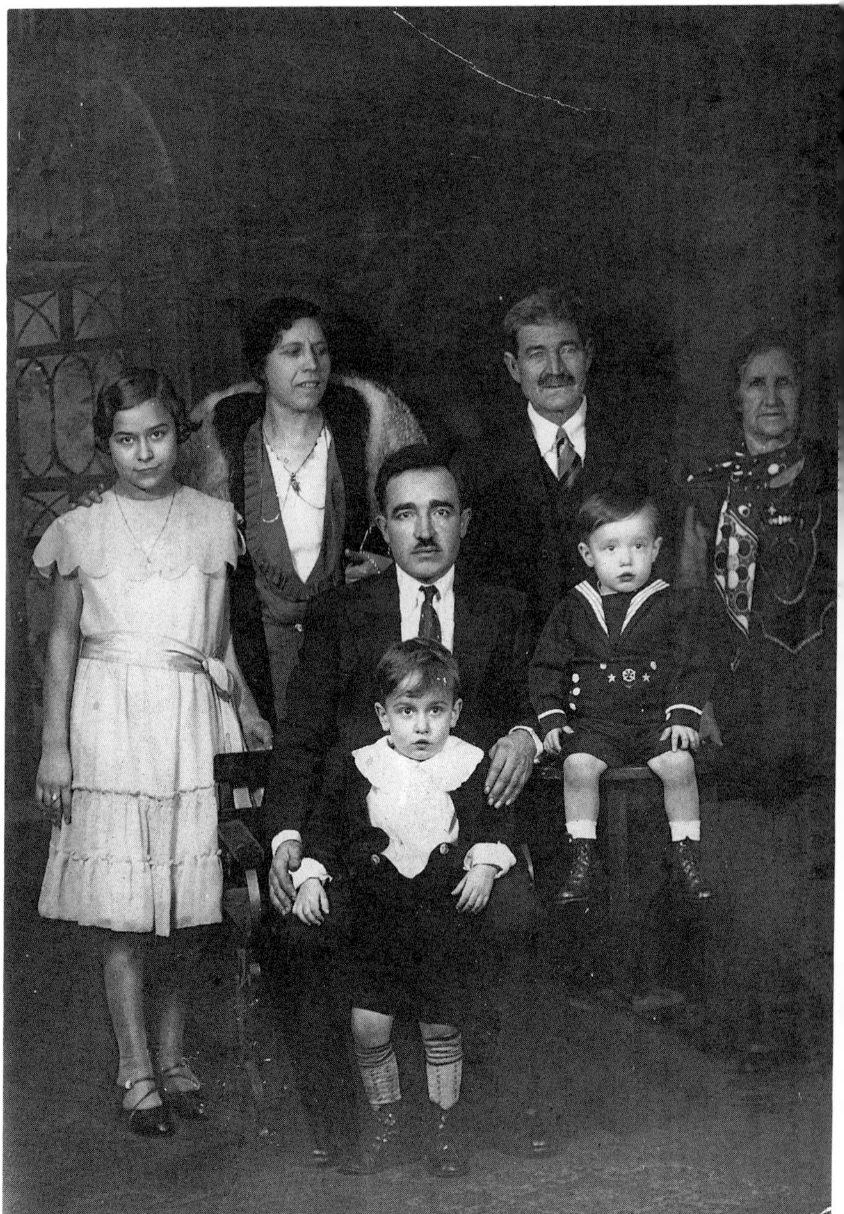

Hands On, Not Hands Out

More elitist dribble to report: You know those remarkably tolerant individuals, free of any and all biases. They're tolerant all right, except for those who desire maintaining a quality of life in this country by bringing a little bit of sanity into our immigration laws. Former Governor Richard Lamm of Colorado has said, "When the bathtub is overflowing, you turn off the spigot." *Right on...*off.

My ancestors didn't cross the Atlantic on the *Mayflower*. Nevertheless, I have the moral right to speak on this issue, especially when I see the nation deteriorating because of out-of-control immigration.

My paternal grandparents emigrated from Italy. My grandfather chose to live in an ethnically-mixed neighborhood, instead of predominantly Italian, because he believed it would help my grandmother learn to speak English more quickly if she couldn't always rely on her Italian. My grandmother went to English classes and not only learned the language of America, but she chose never to return to Italy. *America was her home.* My aunt, who was six-years-old when she came to these shores, was placed in a New York City public school, not knowing a word of the language. She learned

English without a bilingual tutor or catering bureaucracy. The assimilation process worked without thwarting their *Italianism.*

My maternal grandparents were first generation Americans. My grandmother could still speak German, her parents having emigrated from Austria. They put down roots in an area known as the *Slate Belt* in Pennsylvania. The small town of Bangor, surrounded by working slate quarries and cornfields, was a stark contrast to the Bronx.

I can say that I'm rooted in the Bronx, but feel fortunate to have gotten a taste of *small town America.* In the Bronx it was homemade ravioli, minestrone soup, and broccoli and spaghetti. In Bangor it was meat-pie for supper and shoo-fly pie for dessert. From the Bronx to Bangor, it tasted good.

With all my grandparents gone now, I am acutely aware of the void created by their passing. Theirs was not a generation dependent on government, nor was it seeking redress for being economically-disadvantaged--as many were. *It was the attitude, stupid,* that made their stories, more times than not, success stories.

The Italian immigrants weren't exactly welcomed with open arms. Ask Mario Cuomo. He gets the first part of his immigrant story right, but doesn't draw the obvious conclusion. *He made it.* And during World War I, the Irish told my "Hun" grandmother, then a ten-year-old girl, to go back to Germany, even though she was born in Pennsylvania, and her parents were from Austria.

The Lazarus Woman

On October 28, 1886, French sculptor Frederic-Auguste Bartholdi's 151-foot high bronze "Statue of Liberty" was dedicated in New York Harbor. It was a generous 100-year-old birthday gift from the French government, celebrating the centennial of American independence. President Grover Cleveland presided over the pomp. The inscription on the Statue was from poet Emma Lazarus' *The New Colossus.*

That was then...*this is now.* At the turn of the 20th century, America's population was 75 million. Today it's 265 million, and growing. In 1900, the Industrial Revolution was the rage. Factories had more jobs to fill than qualified applicants. There were wide open spaces in abundance. The environment wasn't yet laden with toxic dumps and acid rain.

Back then, immigrants sought to become Americans and assimilate into the broader culture. They viewed America as not just a place to live, but as *a place to love.* Multi-culturalism occurred naturally--but in the confines of *one* American culture.

There was no welfare colossus circa 1900 America. Émigrés were often compelled to take low-paying jobs in horrific work places. *But they did.*

Immigration today has been poisoned by the modern welfare state and Affirmative Action. We now live in a crybaby society, where too many people believe that the government owes them something. Witness the fast and furious rush to citizenship when the welfare reform bill, impacting on immigrants' government monies, was passed.

Mine Eyes Have Seen...

The supreme function of statesmanship is to provide against preventable evils.
Those who knowingly shirk it, deserve, and not infrequently receive, the curses of those who come after.
- Enoch Powell, on immigration, 1968

In 1993 President Clinton appointed a presidential commission to study the immigration problem and report back to him. Heading the commission was former congresswoman Barbara Jordan. When she, and the other prominent Americans on the panel, recommended a cut in the flow of legal immigrants by 30%, it fell on deaf ears. Even though their findings showed that our excessively generous immigration policies were adversely impacting on American jobs, Congress and the President did nothing. The fatuous First Lady even touted increasing the immigration numbers.

There Used To Be A Good Neighborhood Right Here

Immigration-fueled population growth, which is expected to make Florida the third largest state ahead of New York in the next twenty years, will outstrip the state's ability to provide education, transportation, and protect its environment. To maintain the current school student/building ratios, for example, means that the state will have to build a new school every five days on average for the next twenty-five years.
- from a Center for Immigration Studies report, Shaping Florida: The Effect of Immigration-- 1970-2020

It's easy for journalists like Morton Kondracke to smugly champion the current levels of immigration. And it's easy for his ilk to suggest that those with legitimate concerns about the negative impact of our present immigration laws are nativists, xenophobes, and racists. The Kondrackes in the media, who live in their *Cocktail Communities*, haven't a clue.

The Bronx, not too long ago, was a great place to live (contrary to its *Fort Apache* reputation). There were many fine neighborhoods. Steadily, over the past few decades, many of these livable neighborhoods have fallen under the weight of an immigrant influx that has sent the middle-class packing.

Former mayor of New York City, and *patrician poster boy*, John V. Lindsay, says that he believes the city will "come back," when "the non-poor return from the suburbs." *What are they going to return to, Mr. L?* If nothing is done to reverse the trends of today...*forget about it.* The Third World has arrived and it's not something to celebrate.

If we continue to let in 700,000 and 800,000 legal immigrants a year, on top of the large number of illegals, we can say farewell to America as a nation. *Seeing is believing.*

There's *no* comparison of today's immigration with yesteryear's. It's a vastly different time. Peter Brimelow in *Alien Nation* writes that "immigration must be treated as a luxury for the United States, not as a necessity."

Right you are, Peter.

Give Me Your Tired, Your Poor...Not!

...Give me your tired, your poor
Your huddled masses yearning to breathe free,
The wretched refuse of your teeming shore.
Send these, the homeless, tempest-tost to me,
I lift my lamp beside the golden door!
- Inscription on the base of
The Statue of Liberty

Emma Lazarus' all embracing words are sadly antiquated. Living in New York City, I can say, without hesitation, that we have absorbed enough *wretched refuse.* And the present-day indigent in America are the last people who need more "huddled masses" coming here.

Just look at the New York City public school system and you'll see what our immigration "policies" have wrought. Don't take my word for it, or Mayor Giuliani's contrary position. Come see for yourself. **Beware:** Such a fact-finding tour is not recommended for those with heart conditions, or taking prescription drugs.

Jobs...And Jazz

Give them jobs!
-Zeke

Mario Cuomo on his former "thought radio" program offered a suggestion for a bumper sticker. It should read *"Jobs...Not Jazz,"* he said.

My friend Zeke has said that all of the country's problems could be solved with jobs. Better jobs would solve a lot of problems, but not the kind he was thinking of. Mike Dukakis talked all the time about "good jobs at good wages." *Right on, Mike. But...*

Having seen first hand what the job pool consists of in the New York Metropolitan area, I think another problem exists, well beyond availability of work. The majority of applicants for both retail entry-level stock and cashier positions and management slots, were not temperamentally and intellectually suited for a job...any job. This sorry fact transcended ethnicity and race.

An *attitude adjustment* is in order. A

check up from the neck up. I worked alongside many a young person who referred to his mother's "boyfriend" or his father's "wife." It used to be that your father's wife was your mother.

I'm not casting aspersions on non-traditional families...*okay, so I am!* Just emphasizing that it's not solely a question of jobs.

Unless I've been sold a bogus bill of goods, my immigrant grandparents and their generation valued whatever jobs they could get.

Perhaps the area which I've called home my entire life is not representative of America-at-large. But there's a lot of truth to the fact that many people are incapable of holding a job...period.

Mario wants jobs, not jazz.
Who doesn't?

Murder, He Wrote

This is the saddest commentary on the America we live in. I'm talking about the fate of a brutal double-murderer named O.J. Simpson. He's not only a free man, but he's been *feted* in parts of the black community. *Feted for what?* For beating his wife senseless when he was married to her, or for nearly decapitating her in a vicious, bloody assault after their split?

For the generation before me, their most remembered moment in American history is the assassination of JFK. Where were you when you first got the news that the President had been killed? My father heard the news from a neighbor when he was heading to work. He only knew there had been a shooting. When he arrived at work, it was official: Kennedy was dead. Most of the guys, my father recalled, concerned themselves with the prospect of getting the following day off. *(They did.)*

Oh, how we've degenerated. Now most of us have retained the coordinates of when we heard the O.J. Simpson Verdict. I was working the floor of a pet food store called Pet Nosh when the news came in. The *soft rock* music station, that was being piped through the store, interrupted its regular programming for the breaking news.

I noticed a couple of black women patrons on the premises, who stopped their shopping along with everyone else. Something told me to head for the backroom.

Of course when the chilling **NOT GUILTIES** were read, the black women were whooping it up--*screaming with joy.* It was one of the most offensive scenes I'd ever witnessed. And I was ensconced behind an *Employees Only* glass door. Yet I could hear their *twisted glee* through thick glass.

This moment crystallized in my mind the state of race relations in America. To protest the verdict, I, along with a few co-workers, briefly considered burning down Pet Nosh and participating in a full blown *Day of Rage.* As we looked out upon Central Avenue in Yonkers, we thought about flagging down a truck and beating its driver to a pulp.

Surprise of surprises: We didn't.

Celebrating Perversity

Rickles is not for the thin-skinned or the socially
conscious....(His humor was) directed at
individuals or groups who had no need
to feel threatened by the jibes....
(I)t was distasteful and uncomfortable when
Rickles, a white comedian, led an overwhelmingly
European-American audience down the path of
verbal Arabic, Asian, and
African-American bashing.

---A review of a Don Rickles' performance at the
Cape Cod Melody Tent on 8/11/96
from the *Cape Cod Times*.
(Having attended the show, where Rickles called
Americans of Italian ancestry "greaseballs," Irish,
"boozers," and Germans, "Nazis,"
I can only assume the reviewer, Joe Burns,
must have been suffering from
incontinence that night.)

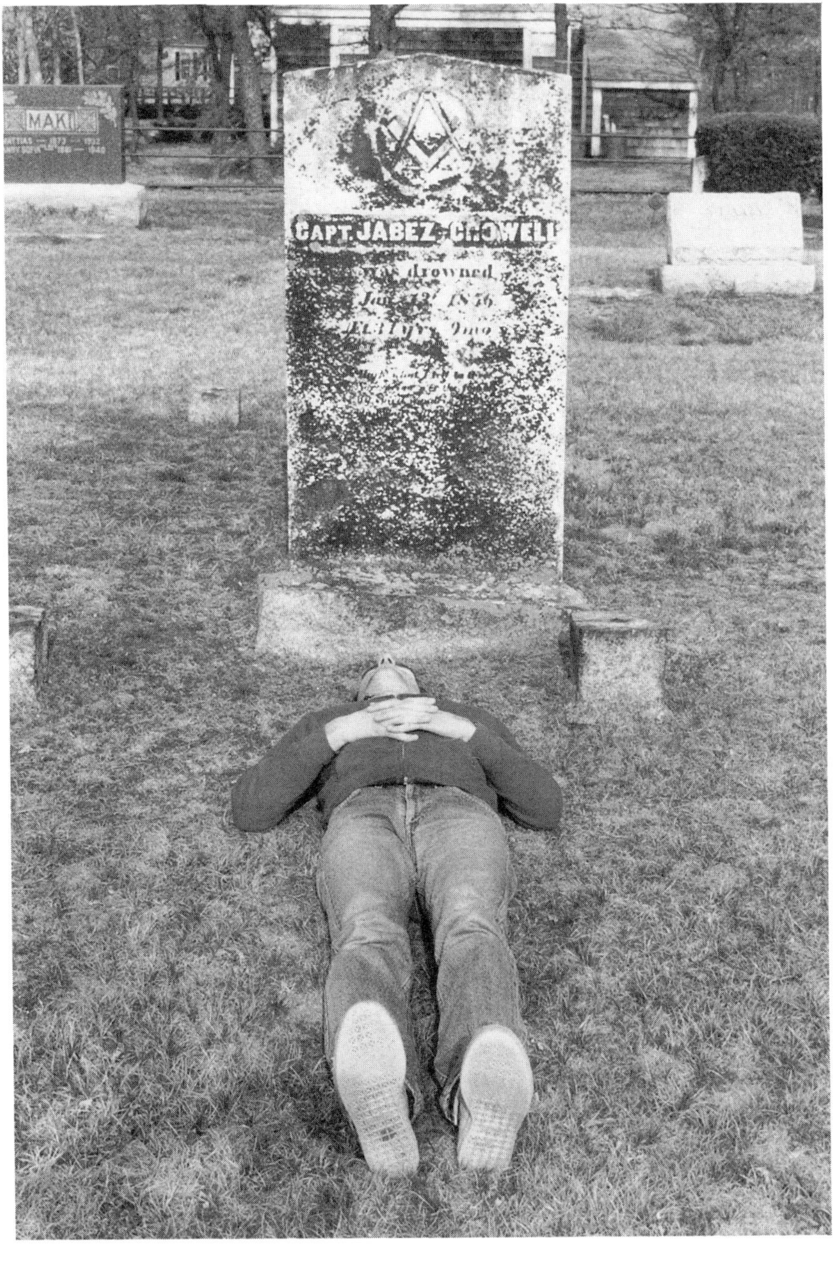
MAKI
CAPT. JABEZ
was drowned

Boorish On America

Are we in North America?
- a confused bookstore cashier to a colleague,
about to ring up a magazine with
two prices on it--one listed in
British pounds for the UK,
and the other in dollars for North America.

The most egregious assault on America has occurred in the classroom--from kindergarten to college. Politically correct swine have infiltrated the America educational structure and cast a net of mediocrity over it.

The new national *Standards for the English Language Arts* talks about "word identification strategies." *Reading.* Reading is now on par with every possible form of expression. Graffiti on a subway car is as legitimate an art form as Manet or Monet. Watching an episode of *Saved by the Bell* is as much of an accomplishment as reading *War and Peace.* After all, a child must search for his own meaning. Let him go see *Independence Day* and perhaps his "different writing process elements" will surface. For God's sake, let's not get in the way of a kid's "alternate expressions." And a little "personal spelling" never hurt anyone, did it?

This trend towards no (albeit, oh so sensitive) standards does not bode well for the future. The technologically-explosive 21st century beckons the youth of today. The very same youngsters who are not afforded those incidental "prescribed sequences" called *reading, writing, and arithmetic.*

When some schools advance essay writing where "inventive spelling" is encouraged--something's not *kosher.* When educators reason that correcting misspelling is tantamount to impeding creativity--**nah!**

Once upon a time graduating from high school meant that you could actually read and write. In this *Age of Enlightenment*, higher education is considered a birthright, even if you are a moron and/or lunkhead.

Standards.... These days, setting them in schools or the work place is considered either racially-motivated or cruel and unusual punishment, or just plain mean.

Bowls 2000

I know what it's like to be in a wheelchair, without having been in one--unlike yourself!
-Zeke

The Americans With Disabilities Act is a law for the 1990s. I thought it was a great idea at the time of its passage. So did George Bush, Bob Dole, and Ted Kennedy.

The law sounded good, fair, and compassionate. Opposing it was political suicide and a sound byte disaster. An ambitious politician could not cross the physically-challenged lobby.

Now, reality has set in, and small businesses in particular are shouldering the burden of compliance with this *compassionate* piece of legislation.

Having priority parking spaces for the disabled makes a lot of sense. There are numerous people on wheels that shop and visit office complexes who should not have to park in the boon docks. But why should the federal government involve itself in telling businesses that they have to have these spots? A media campaign from interested organizations would do the trick. *The American Way.*

Having been involved on the periphery of a small business, I got a taste of the burdensome red tape that is *The Americans With Disabilities Act.*

Case in point. A retail outlet was purchased with one bathroom on the premises. It was up a short flight of stairs. This was against the law. By law, a new bathroom should have been built. It wasn't. Sometimes an inefficient bureaucracy comes in handy.

Same store. With six cash register stations on site, the owners were legally required to handicap-equip (lower) them. *Ever see a cashier in a wheelchair?*

> *Create something for other people...*
> *and I'm all for it.*
> *- Zeke*

After dining at a restaurant on Cape Cod, I visited the men's room and noticed a lonely toilet bowl, looking quite forlorn. Gone was the stall that used to afford the *bowlers* a bit of privacy. Apparently it was the cheapest way for this eatery to comply with cumbersome government regulations. Rather than build a separate facility with handicap access, the restaurateur removed the stall.

Fortunately, I didn't have to visit the bowl. (Foreign bowls are an absolute last resort for me.) And the urinal is a contraption not as enmeshed in government regulations as is the hapless toilet bowl.

As we approach the *Millennium*, it behooves us to get accustomed to *Bowls 2000* as our privacy gets flushed away and business costs skyrocket. Business costs=consumer costs.

The main beneficiaries of this stinking climate are the lawyers, not the disabled.

Don't forget to flush.

Baseball Has Been Very, Very Good To Me

Baseball used to be our national pastime. Used to be. Our cultural demise is no better epitomized than in the plunge in popularity of this once great game.

From the fans in the stands to the announcers in their booths; from the greedy, short-sighted owners, to the boorish, selfish players on the field, baseball ain't what it was. *Not by a long shot.*

Baseball is the only sport that ever interested me as a fan. My team, for over twenty-five years, has been the *New York Mets*. My father was a die-hard *Yankees* fan and so my first baseball fan experiences occurred in the old Yankee Stadium, literally the *House That*

Ruth Built. We used to make the ten-minute drive from home to the stadium and park a few blocks away on the street. (It wasn't that my father was cheap and didn't want to pay for parking. Rather, he had a strong aversion to traffic jams and getting out of parking lots. I've inherited this gene.) Today, that once decent area surrounding the stadium is not as hospitable, both for people and their automobiles. The *Stadium Motor Lodge*, not too far from the ballpark, which always intrigued me as a kid with its giant baseball marquee, is now The *Stadium Family Center.* Hmmm....

About twenty minutes from Yankee Stadium, across the Triborough Bridge, is where my baseball thrills and letdowns were had. Shea Stadium. A stadium built in the shadow of La Guardia Airport. Whereas twenty years ago, the only distractions in the place were the ascending and descending jet planes; today it's loud, obnoxious rock music blared over the public address system, and a bigger than ever share of beer-brained inebriates spewing a vile bile not fit for sore ears. Gone is the traditional organ music that used to complement *the summer game.*

Shea Stadium is no anomaly. The organ music and baseball marriage just doesn't cut it anymore. Baseball, the game, is suddenly too boring for the masses, who have to have their brains stimulated with something that can only loosely be called music. Obviously, today's "fans" aren't particularly interested in baseball.

A former *New York Mets* outfielder named Vince Coleman, being paid over three million dollars a year, admitted to *never having heard of Jackie Robinson.* Coleman, a black man, was unaware of the *Brooklyn Dodgers'* player that paved the way for blacks in the major leagues. Robinson went through *holy hell* as a pioneer in the National League, being taunted and threatened in cities everywhere. Coleman, like so many of today's ballplayers and "fans," is absent a historical perspective.

When I was ten-years-old, the *Mets* brought back Willie Mays to finish his career in New York, where it had started over twenty years before with the long-departed *Giants.* It was a magical sports moment. Willie Mays was a legendary sports figure, and even though he was past his prime with little left in his forty-year-old body, us young fans understood what he meant to the game and to its history. Today, old-timers games, showcasing the greats and not-so-greats of the past, are almost extinct. This past *All-Star Classic* saw a traditional old-timers game ditched in favor of an *MTV Celebrity Softball Game.*

Gone too are most of the great voices of the game. Lindsay Nelson, my personal favorite announcer from yesteryear, painted the word picture with knowledge of the game and modest enthusiasm. One of his successors in the broadcast booth is a man named Tim McCarver, considered the *announcer for the 90s.*

McCarver over-analyzes every managerial move and play on the field and is often critical. "That's a bad move," he sneers. "I don't understand that!" he has been heard to say over and over. Apparently the fan of today, hooked on analysis and psycho-babble, or just plain dumb, wants to be lectured, even when watching a baseball game. Lindsay Nelson and his contemporaries described the happenings on the field with rich voices and a perspective. The fans decided for themselves if a manager was a "bozo" or a player a "loafer."

And now the baseball owners want to expand further, and further dilute the limited talent that exists in the game. This, on top of the game's declining grip on America's psyche, portends bad things for the sport that once was just like *Apple Pie* and *Motherhood.*

Balls in the Hood

A final thought on baseball in America--particularly in the cities. During the summers of my youth in the 1970s, baseball-oriented activity was still the rage. We played hardball in Van Cortlandt Park, stickball in the streets and off the local high school's wall, whiffleball in our concrete backyards, and stoopball off our stoops. There was punchball, kickball, and box baseball--all variations of the only game that counted during the dog days. On these same streets today, I see very little baseball in any form. I don't see kids doing anything for that matter.

My father and his friends played stickball in the same streets I walk across today. Many of the guys in those days played the game in pleated suit pants and dress shoes. There were no $150 Nikes in the 40s.

We've come a long way....

A Tough Nut to Crack

For over a decade, us Kingsbridge residents have had our very own "street person." I'll call him "Ethan" to avoid an *ACLU* lawsuit.

Ethan is mentally challenged...*a nut*. His is a tragic story born of the bottle.

He has loomed around the Chase Manhattan Bank for over a decade, spouting harsh non-sequiturs and twitching his head *a la* Linda Blair in *The Exorcist*. He has turned over a few mailboxes in his day and destroyed their contents. A federal offense, I dare say. Once he jumped into an unattended mail truck and drove it on to the sidewalk and into a storefront.

Despite these criminal acts, Ethan goes unpunished. Because he's a nut, he appears to be *above the law*, even though he is a major *Menace 2 Society*.

Maybe he's really a disgruntled postal worker. I don't know. Just get him off the streets before an innocent pedestrian is flattened by a runaway mail truck.

The Check Republic

I'm a poor man.
I have no right to be fat.

--Sgt. Hanz Schultz,
Hogan's Heroes

We Accept
FOOD
STAMPS

ID REQUIRED
RESTAURANT QUALIFIED ONLY

155 S. BROADWAY — YONKERS

The Ozzie and Harriet Defense League

A Report for the New Millennium:

Be you a candidate for president, or lonely voice of the people, don't talk about the "good old days." Condemnation will come fast and furious from the kind-hearted Left, who look only toward the hopeful future, never back to the *ugly* past.

Their specious argument goes: Do we want to return to the pre-civil rights era? Do we want women in the kitchen? The answer is obviously **NO**, but I don't think that Dr. King desired a trade-off of a more civil time for basic civil rights.

As recently as the early 1980s, the Nigro family often left their door unlocked during daylight hours. Our letter carrier, Louie, who never made his rounds without a cigar between his teeth, would open the front door and put our mail in the hallway. If we smelled a stogie, our mail had arrived.

In this trusting vein, there were no bars on the windows, no *Clubs* or car alarms. Graffiti was shocking vandalism, not a commonplace eyesore.

According to 1965 FBI statistics, there were 137 violent crime arrests per 100,000 juveniles; 532 in 1994.

So, I'd let Ozzie and Harriet rest in peace. There was much repression and ignorance in their day, but I'd hold off on celebrating. There's no reason why we shouldn't be wistful for the bygone days before metal detectors in schools, drive-by shootings, and bullet proof glass protecting *NBC's Today Show.* Dave Garroway and J. Fred Muggs hosted the show in a more civilized age than Bryant Gumbel.

Welfare, You're The Devil

Some of the lowest birthrates in American history occurred during the *Great Depression* years (1929-1940). Before "welfare," and *cash for kids* from the government, it would seem that many families, experiencing financial hard times, behaved responsibly.

It's been demonstrated in Europe (and New Jersey) that more money for more children encourages more irresponsibility from the "moms" cashing welfare checks.

During the endless debates on the role of the federal government in guaranteeing welfare (AFDC) monies to people, the hue and cry revolved around the impact of any new legislation on children.

The children...the *real* victims-of-society. I consider it *child abuse* for women (and their absentee husbands) to have children they cannot afford. A woman having a child she can't provide for, and expecting the working taxpayer to support her and her family, is behaving so irresponsibly, one should immediately question her fitness to be a role model and parent.

What about the children? The welfare behemoth that has consumed America these past thirty years has administered, through a swollen bureaucracy, more cruelty to kids than any cuts in government "benefits" could.

Some political demagogues and their media accomplices will find people, even children, who will no doubt be adversely impacted by the end of welfare *as we know it*. This much is certain. As with any change in law, be it welfare or health care, the safety net's got a few holes in it.

The mainstream press rarely sees the big picture. The long-term gains of breaking the generational dependency on welfare, if it happens, will be dramatic. And while some hard-luck stories will be encountered in the transitional years ahead, how many will be avoided in the future?

You know what, there's plenty of tragic tales to be told right now, courtesy of sorry, short-sighted governmental policies, being administered by peevish pencil-pushers.

Lentil Soup for the Soul

It's always been my understanding that food stamps were devised to give poorer Americans an opportunity for better nutrition. It came as a surprise to me when I noticed that a nearby *McDonald's* was accepting food stamps! And the sign was in English *and* Spanish.

McDonalds isn't cheap; the days of the 19 cent hamburger are long gone. It would cost a minimum of $12 to feed a family of four. And it's *pseudo-food!* That food stamps can be used to buy unhealthy crap is another example of contemporary society's decline.

The federal government is obviously not interested in good nutrition, but I would like to offer my lentil soup recipe to feed a family of four. It's easy to prepare, and good for you too. *Healthy kids make happy kids.*

8 cups water
2 cloves garlic (finely chopped)
2 tablespoons salt
1 basil leaf or pinch of parsley
1 cup lentils
1 cup Acini pepe pasta (or your favorite)

Bring the water and salt to a full boil. Add the lentils, garlic, and seasonings. Simmer for an hour and twenty-five minutes. Add the separately cooked pasta.

This fine fare can feed a family of four. Add a loaf of bread or crackers to the meal, and who could ask for more? Tasty, filling, and healthy. My last bag of lentils cost 69 cents, and this recipe only uses half a bag.

This bean-based diet is inexpensive and far more healthy than a Big Mac.

A little flatulence is a small price to pay for good nutrition.

Christopher Columbus: The Man

Do you celebrate *Indigenous Peoples Day?* Get ready, it might be replacing *Columbus Day* in the near future. Yes, Christopher Columbus, the embodiment of all that is and has been evil. The father of all crimes committed against the colorful little people of the world since 1492.

In my college days, I got on a Columbus-kick. I've been on other such kicks (*Watergate*, Lincoln, TV character actors, religious fundamentalists, and a long-dead neighbor lady that drank like a fish and looked like a vampire). I read several biographies of the man and researched his sailing logs. I recall being in awe of him and his courageous exploratory spirit.

It was the 15th century and the earth was thought to be flat, and the sea replete with monsters. Contagious diseases and malnutrition abounded. A little 15th century boat ride was not quite like cruising the high seas on the *Pacific Princess.*

Okay, so Columbus was no *Captain Stubing.* Fortunately for us. Columbus was a man with a vision. *Flawed?* Certainly, but a great man of his time.

The "multi-culturalists" who revel in defaming the famous sailor, measure Columbus by *20th century mores.* Odd, isn't it, that the "multiculturalists" who bash the evil and racist West, always use *Western* values and ethics as their rulers. Granted, Columbus wouldn't be a viable political candidate in the 1990s. But...

How come the "multiculturalists" don't hold today's Third World despots to 20th century Western ethics? They don't even hold them to *15th century Western ethics.*

Columbus has been snatched out of his time and been found Guilty in the court of "multi-cultural" opinion.

He's in good company.

Pardon Me For Not Celebrating Diversity

I'm not of a mind to pop the champagne bottle for the dissolution of America as a nation-state. So, you'll pardon me for not *celebrating diversity*.

"Diversity" and "multi-culturalism" are insidious wedges that have crept into the American body politic; wedges designed to tear America apart.

All too many politicians have capitulated to this national constipation of rational thought and are undermining the oneness that binds our nation. Pity the United States of America if this virus isn't purged.

Now is the time for our nation to take a fifty-state dose of acidophilus and let the diarrhea called "diversity" and "multi-culturalism" discharge.

Dream Away

The liberals can understand everything but people who don't understand them.

-- Lenny Bruce

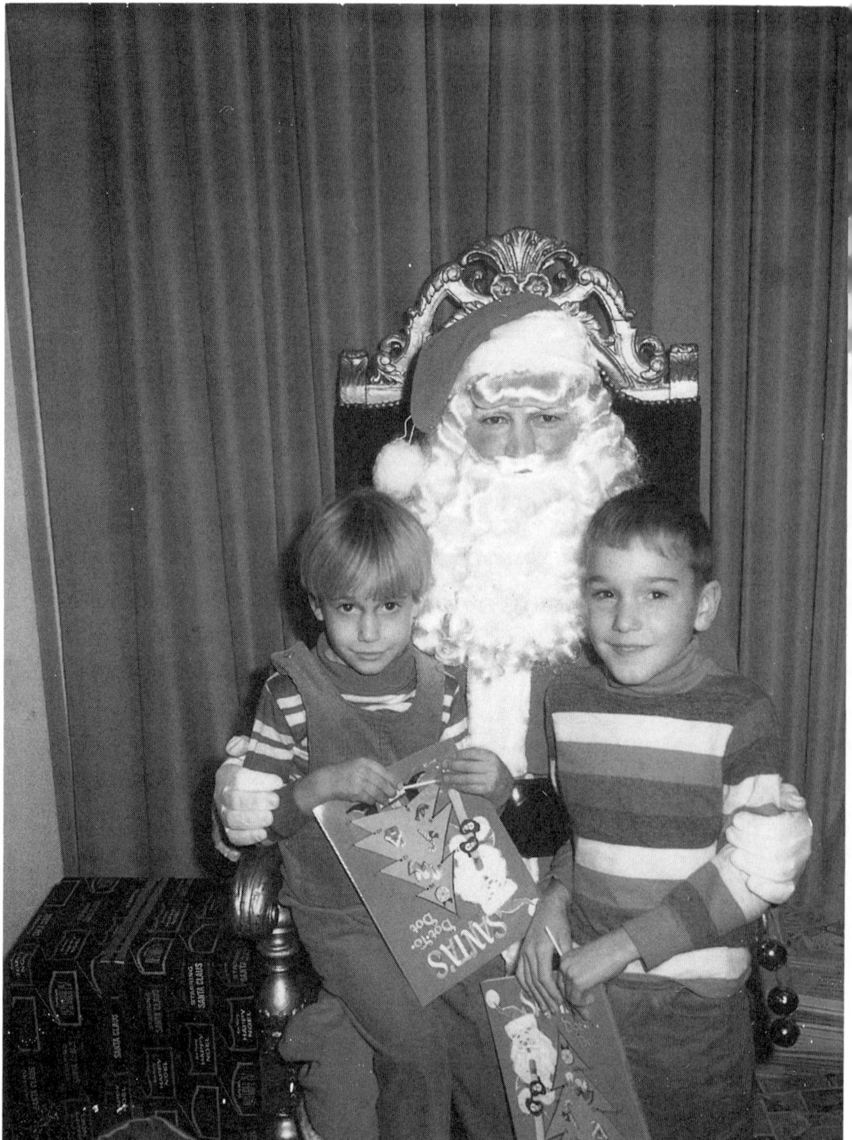
SANTA'S
Dot-To-Dot

__Dream Along With Me:__
__A Wish List__

I wish that:

The judiciary would stop behaving like the legislature. The judiciary of the late 20th century, from the federal on down, is composed of too many judges with political agendas. The only literal interpretation of the *Constitution* these judges recognize is their *lifetime tenure.*

A **NO SNEERING BEYOND THIS POINT** placard was boldly displayed at the most common entry points for today's immigrants. Remember the early century news footage of immigrants approaching Ellis Island and waving, en masse, their American flags. *Cheers, not jeers* was the order of that day.

Equality of opportunity, regardless of race, sex, or creed, actually meant it. Then West Point cadet Hayley Ulrich wouldn't be at West Point. She'd be in the school she always wanted to go to, the University of California at Berkeley. You see, based on her grades and achievement level in high school, she was more deserving than half of those that were admitted to the university, but was passed over in favor of students that would add "diversity" to the student body.

The IRS would go the way of the 1970s leisure suit.

All future tax increases had to be approved by the *vox populi.*

There were term limits on all political jobs. This just might up the odds that a pol, or two, might do what's in the best interest of Americans, instead of what's politically expedient.

Section Eight eligible families were permitted to move into Peter Jenning's Manhattan apartment building.

Eleanor Clift would come clean and admit she gets aroused when she sees the President. Or is it the First Lady? Perhaps both.

For every new law passed in this country, be it federal, state, or local, two were stricken from the books. Ditto: regulations.

New York City cab drivers actually knew how to drive. And that they were made aware of a recent invention called soap.

Public school aficionados, who vehemently oppose school choice vouchers would, at least, send their kids to the public schools they champion. If not: *Sh-uuu-t Uuu-p.*

<u>Dishonorable Mention</u>

<u>Ann Lewis</u>
Do you ever learn anything new from this woman? She's dredged up time and again by the networks to give her partisan spin on things. Stop it, please! A final word on Ann: She's Congressman Barney Frank's sister. *Where did their parents go wrong?*

<u>Jerry Springer</u>
The top knave of trash TV is the former mayor of the *Queen City.* A man who resigned from public office when it was revealed that he kept company with a call girl in a Kentucky motel, and paid her with a personal check. *Final Thought, Jerry: You're not only a sleazeball, you're also stupid.*

<u>JFK, Jr.</u>
The dullard with *helmet hair* from America's most annoying family. I wish he had stayed on his step-dad's Greek island, or moved to nearby Nicosia instead of the *Big Apple.* This would have spared us countless front-page stories on

his failed bar exams and various tiffs with the distaff set.

Bill Press
Michael Kinsley's replacement on *Crossfire*. A marginal improvement, but another weak-mouthed elitist who thinks *Big Brother* knows best....

Sally Jesse Raphael
She had the temerity to use the *Radio Hall of Fame* awards to bash Rush Limbaugh for calling some women *feminazis*. Ms. Raphael can host a show with topics such as *Hermaphrodite Masturbation Techniques* and still consider herself a societal treasure and role model. Rush just happens to be funny, something foreign to Sally Jessy.

Donna Shalala
The Queen of the Speech Code. Try this one on for size, Miss Shalala: *You're a fly speck on a mound of doggie-doo.*

Jack Kemp
Big disappointment. He is not ready for prime time. Forget *Kemp 2000*, Jack. You didn't want to deal with the "wedge issues," of immigration and Affirmative Action. It's not the issues that

create the wedge, it's the policies. I can't stand any more of your gushing cheerfulness, masking a disturbing think-tank elitism.

Mario Cuomo Looks Like a Frog.... and other observations

Aside from his resemblance to the cigar-chomping *Frog* from *Courageous Cat & Minute Mouse*, Mario will be remembered for presiding over a state in perpetual decline. During the 1990-91 national recession, one out of every three people who lost their jobs were New Yorkers. The *Empire State* shouldered the highest tax burden in the country, and state spending doubled.

New York Daily News staff writer Robert Dominguez, commenting on Leonel Fernandez' election as president of the Dominican Republic, wrote that "Fernandez is as much a symbol of the American Dream as he is an immigrant success story." Are *American Dreams* now to be elected presidents of foreign countries?

Approximately 40% of Social Security payments go to oldsters who make more than the national median income. FDR said the purpose of Social Security was to prevent "poverty-ridden old age."

Of Pressing Concern

You gave it to me to warm me,
but it has kept me too hot.

-- Last words uttered by
Stanislas I, King of Poland, in 1766,
referring to the bathrobe he requested which caught fire,
causing fatal burns.

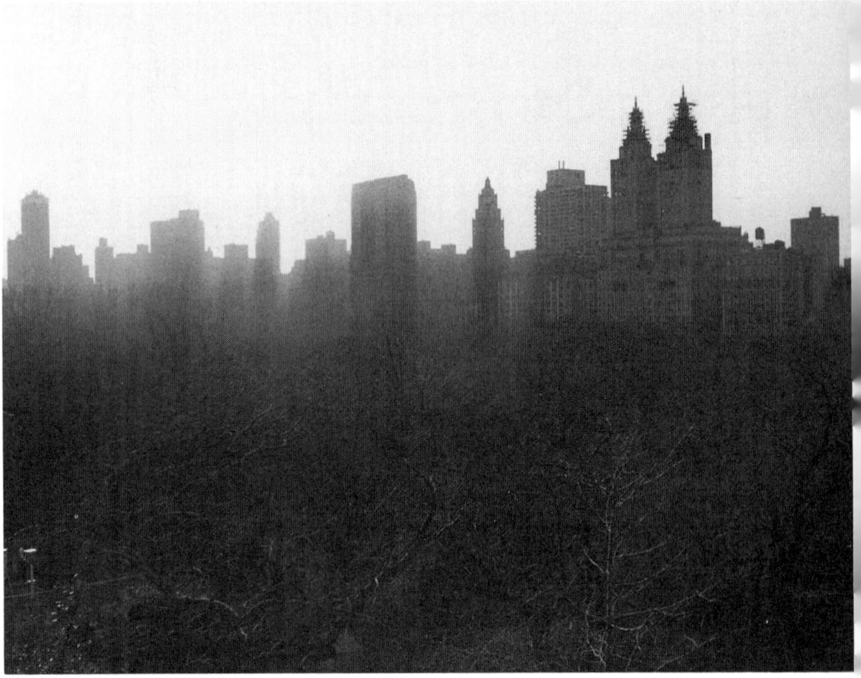

Are You Going To Watch Scarborough on Four?

Local television newsman, Chuck Scarborough of *WNBC* in New York, was castigated by the print media, and taken to the woodshed by his bosses, for giving a campaign contribution to a Republican presidential candidate.

When the *Steve Forbes for President* donor list was made public, the newsman's name was on it. It became public knowledge that Scarborough had given $1,000 to the affably goofy multi-millionaire who was bankrolling his own campaign.

No big deal, except to the hypocritical media minions who expressed outrage that a reporter, who was supposed to be "fair," had the audacity to exercise a First Amendment right. *WNBC* went so far as to bar Scarborough from reporting on any political stories.

On their high horse, the media barrage continued, claiming that Scarborough had committed a major and inexcusable *faux pas* for a newsman. Would these sanctimonious elites have been as condemnatory if, it had been discovered, Scarborough had given money to *Clinton-Gore?*

And what's this impartial dictate that

Scarborough supposedly violated by giving money to Forbes? Does this act alone reveal an inherent bias in Scarborough's character and ability to report fairly? Maybe, but...

Sam Donaldson, owner of a 27,000 acre ranch in New Mexico, has played pundit on *This Week With David Brinkley* and elsewhere. He imparts an obvious political predisposition to his audiences. So, he hasn't actually revealed his voting predilections. We know enough. Donaldson's a very wealthy man, ensconced in the Beltway culture of Washington, DC, who looks down on the Average American peon. As far as Donaldson is concerned, his view of the world is *the* view of the world.

And the same goes for Leslie Stahl, Eleanor Clift, Al Hunt, et al. The vociferous Clift of *Newsweek*, and ubiquitous talking head-pundit, spews her opinions *ad nauseam*. Nobody has been better shill for Bill and Hillary. So what if she didn't give money to their campaigns....

Leave Chuck alone. He's exhibited more on-the-air class than most of the boobs who decried his base crime of making a political contribution.

Buchanan Fodder

He's been compared to Mussolini, Attila the Hun, and the demon of all-time, Adolph Hitler. He's none other than Pat Buchanan, long-time co-host of *Crossfire*, and the man that started an epidemic of apoplexy by winning a mere quarter of the Republican party primary vote in the tiny state of New Hampshire.

You'd have thought he'd been elected dictator. Frothing at the mouth, while trying to win political points by displaying their disgust at a victory for "intolerance" were Mayor Giuliani, former Mayor Koch, and Al *(Shall I be a liberal or a conservative today?)* D'Amato.

Giuliani went ballistic *(what else is new!)*, calling Buchanan a "racist" and "xenophobe." He blasted the former *CNN* pundit for having said, "New York used to be a great town--now look at it." Buchanan had attended the Columbia School of Journalism in Manhattan in the 1960s, when the city was a wholly different and better place.

Not to pass up a chance in the spotlight, former Mayor Ed Koch told his legions of *Ed Heads* that "Pat Buchanan is doing exactly what Adolph Hitler did in 1922...what he is doing is appealing to those deep-rooted horrible sentiments."

Although I would have found it near-impossible to vote for Buchanan, courtesy of his extreme and obsessive abortion position and his penchant for defending geriatric ex-Nazis, I found his 96 candidacy refreshing. He said what he meant and meant what he said--*unheard of in modern politics.*

Buchanan was the only politician talking about things that mattered--like immigration, middle-class job insecurity, and wage stagnation. He tapped into genuine fears about the future of America. Is this a crime?

Giuliani, at his hyperventilating-grandstanding worst, suggested that Buchanan visit the Bushwick section of Brooklyn and the Haitian-immigrant community there, and Flushing, Queens, with its dominant Korean-immigrant population. The Mayor claimed to believe this would disabuse Buchanan of his "anti-immigration" philosophy.

Please....

And Ed Koch wasn't through with Buchanan. For weeks on his *Whine and Spectator* radio program he warned, in his patented hyperbolic style, of this Hitler in our midst.

Comparing a personally-liked, albeit controversial columnist and commentator, to a mass-murdering tyrant is specious and, in Koch's favorite word, an "outrage."

Indeed, Buchanan became a favorite target for politicians, the media, and anybody looking to prove their love for mankind.

A local radio program host, a conservative black man, went into a diatribe about Buchanan's oft-quoted statement that one million Englishmen would be more easily assimilated into the state of Virginia than would one million Zulus. He said he was highly insulted at such obvious bigotry.

Highly insulted at something so obviously self-evident, too.

Message for Michael

While on the subject of Buchanan and *Crossfire*, I would be remiss if I didn't comment on the liberal commentators on the show.

In my liberal daze, I was regularly exasperated with the left-wing hosts, beginning with the cadaverous Tom Braden. He was no match for the energetic Buchanan, and seemed to be doing his utmost to keep his dentures from flying across the studio. I was pleased when he was replaced--*until I saw his replacement.*

What is it about Michael Kinsley? How did this man make it to television? Now, I know about looking bad on camera (see the *Bernie Geotz Debate*), but nobody has offered me a nightly pundit job on nationwide TV.

I found Michael Kinsley a repulsive creature the first day I laid eyes on him, and I began to root for his combative, but human counterpart, Pat Buchanan, and found myself agreeing with him more times than not.

Kinsley, like so many left-leaning, elitist pundits, has a bloodless quality to him. When Dinesh D'Souza and the subject of his book, *The End of Racism*, were debated on *Crossfire*, Kinsley threw a tizzy and *appeared to be holding his breath.* He branded D'Souza's scholarly tome "racist" in the midst of his childish snit. Kinsley was blinded by his guilt at being a white male making a lot of money.

Here's my theory: Kinsley is not a white male after all. He's a descendant from the alien ship that crashed in Roswell, New Mexico in 1947.

The Beginning Of The End

Crito, I owe a cock to Aesculapius; do not forget to pay it.

--Last words of Socrates, to a buddy.

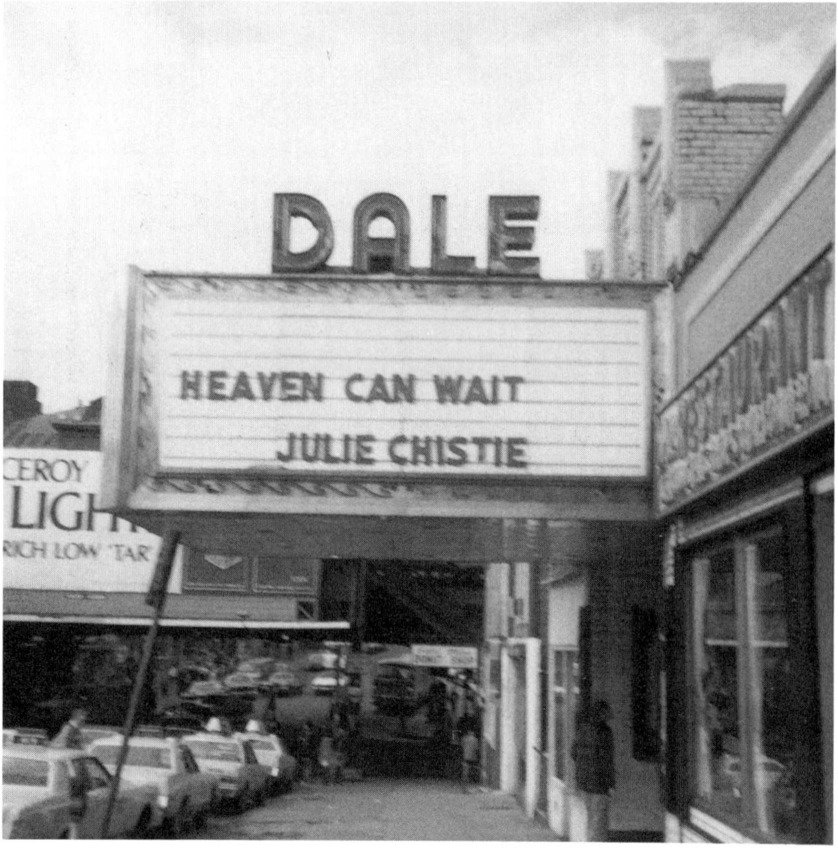
DALE
HEAVEN CAN WAIT
JULIE CHISTIE
CEROY
LIGH
RICH LOW "TAR"

Can't See The Forest and the Trees

I registered as a Democrat because I believed it was the party of ideas. I believed it was the party of the little guy; the party of compassion *(that word again!)*. But now it's time to own-up to the well-intentioned failures of the *Great Society* and its offshoots spanning thirty years.

I asked my life-long Republican father in 1984, how he could be voting for Ronald Reagan's re-election, considering the President's environmental policy positions. Interior Secretary James Watt and Anne Burford, head of the Environmental Protection Agency, were no friends of the environment, no friends of conservation.

Dad said, "You expect me to vote for someone on one issue?"

Today, I can understand where he was coming from. Mike Dukakis had a Boston Harbor problem and Bill Clinton, a chicken dung problem. These guys were the enviro-candidates, whom I supported.

I'm a card-carrying member of the *Nature Conservancy*, I'll admit. I believe in environmental causes. But I try to see the big picture. So many issues impact on the state of the environment.

This should come as no surprise by now, but I believe that a bigger population means more environmental crises. Our population would stabilize around its present level of 265 million if we had sane immigration laws. The more our population grows, the more stresses there are on our air and water quality, and the more open space we lose to development. This is indisputable logic. Ted Kennedy can talk until he's blue in his puffy face on the environment, but if he welcomes a population of 400 million people in fifty years, I don't consider him much of an environmentalist.

The Democratic party does not have a monopoly on environmental protection. Vice President Gore, as a matter-of-fact, has demagogued enviro-issues to death. Robo-Veep has so politicized the debate, it's hard to know what's fact from fiction.

Still, there's a conservative faction that loves to lambaste environmentalists as if they all belong to an extremist monolith. There are crazies out there, worried more about roaches than people. But it's ludicrous to tar so many people, of all political persuasions, who happen to care about over-development, acid rain, clean air and water, and species extinction.

<u>Final Thought</u>

In the fall of 1972, my hip, progressive parochial grammar school introduced a course called *Family Life*. The parents of the fifth-graders were given a chance to peruse the textbook and decide whether to permit their child to take the "sex ed" class. Only four moms (from my observation, they make these decisions) in the entire grade opted out of *Family Life.*

Mrs. Nigro, Mrs. Mannion (my editor's mother) and two others said no, simultaneously saying yes to having their kids join Sr. Therese in a converted broom closet to discuss *situational values*, while our peers learned about *the birds and the bees.* Twenty-five years later, I'm happy to report, the only female in the foursome is the proud mother of a bouncing baby girl. Apparently, she got hold of the *Family Life* book on the sly.

Little did our mothers realize that our own family Bibles were chock full of dicey stuff. *(Catholics rarely read the Bible.)* I was required to purchase *The New American Bible* in Cardinal Spellman High School. Today, I see my name written inside: *Nick Nigro, 1J-310, Fr. Mulligan, rm. 210.*

This is also in that book:

"You shall not approach a woman to have

intercourse with her while she is unclean from menstruation. You shall not have carnal relations with your neighbor's wife, defiling yourself with her... You shall not have carnal relations with an animal, defiling yourself with it; nor shall a woman set herself in front of an animal to mate with it; such things are abhorrent."
(Leviticus 18:19-20,23)

What's my point? Good advice, Leviticus! In those *BC days*, the masses needed such guidance. Incest and the eating of winged insects were commonplace. Two thousand years later, where do we stand in the depravity department?

Since the days of leprosy and scall, we've made a few strides. There is room for optimism. But with the amoral elites running amok in positions of "moral" authority, our future looks bleak. We desperately need a contemporary Leviticus for some additional guidance.

New Age sage Stuart Smalley *(in sharp contrast to his alter ego)* says, "Only you can help you." To all aggrieved parties in America clinging to their victim status: **LET GO!** Big government and the thought police are not going to improve your lot.

That's all *I've* got to say.

Cryptic Press Presents

AMERICA OFF-LINE: Reagan to O.J.
by Nicholas J. Nigro & James Mannion
From 1986-1995, the authors published a satirical newlsetter called *The Progressive Pragmatist*. *The Joe Bob Report* called it *"both funny and intelligent...a rare combination."* Read *Confessions* author Nigro, in his *liberal haze days*, pay homage to Mario Cuomo, put in a good word for the Clinton *health plan*, and lambaste Cardinal O'Connor.
6x9 Quality Paperback/160pages
(ISBN 1-887775-01-3) **$12.95**

I'M KIRK, HE'S STUBING:
Classic Television On The Couch
by Nicholas J. Nigro & James Mannion
In the tradition of the Lincoln-Douglas debates, the authors argue the merits of being Captain Kirk vs. Captain Stubing, etc. And that's only the beginning. Such burning questions are answered: Would the O.J. Simpson verdict have been different if Sgt. Joe Friday had been on the case? In this sensitive era, the authors explore Herman Munster's pain as a person of color, etc., etc.
6x9 Quality Paperback/128 pages w/illustrations
(ISBN 1-887775-02-1) **$12.95**

CONFESSIONS OF A LAPSED LIBERAL:
I've Seen The Light
by Nicholas J. Nigro
There once was a liberal named Nick Nigro. He thought the Welfare State was wonderful. He voted for Mondale, Dukakis, then along came Clinton. This breezy memoir-of-sorts traces the author's political awakening.
5x7 Quality Paperback/144 pages w/illustrations
(ISBN 1-887775-41-2) **$11.00**

NURTURE ME, BABY
by James Mannion
Collection of this popular NYC local celebrity and coffeehouse poet's best verse. Irreverent doggerel with occasionally poignant undertones, this accessible rhyme-smith's raving are far removed from the incoherent ramblings that are often confused with art in modern poetical circles.
5.25x8.5 chapbook/36 pages (autographed, limited edition)
A COLLECTOR'S ITEM!
(ISBN 1-887775-06-4) **$4.95**

Cryptic Press titles are available
in most bookstores.

All titles can be purchased directly from
Cryptic Press.

Please add $2.50 s/h for first book.
(.75 each additional)

NYS residents add 8.25% sales tax.

Send orders to:
Cryptic Press
314 West 231st Street, Suite 452
Bronx, NY 10463

Cryptic Press titles (except *NURTURE ME, BABY*)
distributed exclusively to the trade by
BookWorld Services.

Retail credit card orders also accepted. Call
1-800-444-2524